You

too can be

Ideal!

You
too can be
Ideal!

— A Spiritual Approach —

VEDULA V.L.N. MURTHY

Srikunj Sadbhavana Manch
New Delhi

Cataloguing in Publication Data — DK
[Courtsey: D.K. Agencies (P) Ltd. <docinfo@dkagencies.com>]

Murthy, Vedula V. L. N. (Venkata Lakshmi Narasimha), 1954-
You too can be ideal! : a spiritual approach / Vedula V.L.N. Murthy.
p. cm.
Includes bibliographical references (p.).
ISBN 13: 9788182650176
ISBN 10: 8182650178

1. Spiritual life – Hinduism. 2. Self-culture. 3. Conduct of life. I. Title.

DDC 294.544 22

ISBN 13: 978-81-8265-017-6 **ISBN 10:** 81-8265-017-8
First published in India in 2010

Published by:
Srikunj Sadbhavana Manch
'Srikunj', F-52, Bali Nagar
New Delhi - 110 015

Distributed by:
D.K. Printworld (P) Ltd.
Regd. office : *'Srikunj,'* F-52, Bali Nagar
New Delhi - 110 015
Phones : (011) 2545 3975; 2546 6019; *Fax* : (011) 2546 5926
E-mail: indology@dkprintworld.com
Web: www.dkprintworld.com

Foreword

I HAVE known Sri Vedula VLN. Murthy as an engineer and architect for over three decades. On a couple of occasions I sought his advice on the subject of architecture. However when he came to consult me about the book he was writing, I was not a little surprised for I thought that the book was about his specialization. After discussing with him I realized to my utter astonishment that the subject matter of his book was spiritual in nature.

I firmly believe that unless one has accumulated *punyam* in previous births which was brought over to the present one, one cannot have a spiritual bent of mind. We in the modern period rush through life in feverish haste and have no time to stand and stare at the beautiful things that nature has provided. Most of us run after worldly pleasures which can never give us real happiness. Spirituality and inward vision (*antar mukhatvam*) alone give the real bliss which is beyond the senses. One that realizes this and enjoys the eternal bliss shuns materialistic pleasures. It is rightly said that ambition is a sea wave — the more we drink the more we thirst. In this book Sri Murthy gives suggestions about the type of life we should lead and the food we should eat. He believes that our mind is like an elephant that has run amuck.

Sri Murthy offers some suggestions which are simple to follow but yet great and noble. The book has the good and essential quality of readability. The delineation and exposition of difficult topics is done in as lucid a manner as it is analytical.

I congratulate Sri Murthy for this excellent and valuable book and heartily convey my blessings to him and the members of his family for which my age entitles me to.

Kakinada
April 16, 2010

Sri S. Janaki Rama Sastry
(Janaki jani)
Retd. Principal (A.P.Ed.S.)

Preface

PEOPLE are somehow living in this world either in peace or in tension. Depression, frustration and failure are more common experiences of life in these days. No one is spared from experiencing them, though the degree and intensity of experience may vary. In some form at some time, everyone suffers this depression.

Everything in this world is reciprocatory, as was told by scientist Newton in his laws — "for every action there is equal and opposite reaction." If you give something, you get something. The reap is what is sown. Hence it is up to you to select any action good or bad. One is responsible for one's own actions. No one should blame others for their wrong actions or failures. It is one's life one has to live.

Living peacefully depends on how we think and how we were nurtured in our childhood and how we perceive our life situations, etc. Though we are living in this material world there is something beyond this. This is the life-sustaining divine spirit. As we are immersed in our affairs we do not find time to think on this. Also we cannot believe in this as this requires serious and higher level of thinking. Or we blindly follow the spiritual line — what others are doing.

If we accept our divine nature, we will discover that in all of us there is some part of our personality in our deepest inner core, which remains unaffected. It is so secure that nothing can really affect it. This is our divine nature, pure and sacred. We should live a pure and chaste life. Everyone has a scope to carve out one's destiny and reach the goal of life.

There are large number of people who go to places of worship and pray to God, offer money, materials, etc. But they seldom offer their mind and heart. Often we see that people commit mistakes like taking bribe, criticizing others, excessive gossiping, reading unwanted and unnecessary material, wasting time, cheating the people, consuming non-vegetarian food, alcohol, smoking cigarettes, carelessness, hurting others, etc. Does any religion or the God prompt these people to commit such mistakes? Then what is the use of going to worshipping places, if one does not set oneself on the right path? It means such people cheat themselves and do not have trust in their own actions. This is due to ignorance and lack of understanding. One cannot achieve happiness and peace by these means. This is not the way of happy and holistic living. Excess knowledge, skill and power without holiness make human beings devils.

Our education and Science and Technology have developed much nowadays. But Science and Technology has not taught man how to live peacefully. Efforts are made to produce quality products in every field, but the peace to human mind is forgotten. Man is trying to keep the whole world under his control. He became a slave to machines. He is engulfed by selfishness, anger, greed, tensions and stresses. He is not kind enough to mankind, other creatures and nature. Man is destroying the nature on the earth by exploiting it indiscriminately. Though Science and Technology developed well, it is not able to control the natural disasters like floods, cyclones, tidal waves, earthquakes, tsunamis, landslides, mountain eruptions, forest fires, etc. Man also has failed to control the man-made crimes like murders, suicides, wars, terrorism, rapes, etc. Science and Technology is able to give all the comforts to those people who can afford them. Hence the gap between haves and have-nots is widening. But to combat all these situations some solution lies in spirituality through value system.

Advanced civilization must not limit its efforts to Science and Technology alone. We are living in an increasingly complex world. Severe competition makes the people more selfish and money-oriented. Hence awareness of spirituality, culture, philosophy, and humanity brings improvement. In other words, these can be called human values. These keep humans balanced.

Our education must create social awakening for holistic living. It must teach moral, ethical, social and spiritual values to create self-integrated, well-mannered humans. Without this we are no superior to our animals.

Swami Vivekananda roared on this ethical education. He insisted on the need to create life-building, man-making, and character-building education. He said, "we do not need more academic education. We need more value-based education." A person who is morally educated will be better than a morally bankrupt person with high academic qualification.

Some people feel that spiritual time and secular time are different. They feel that if they spend some time in doing *puja* or go to a temple, it is spiritual time and life. After this if they go to their normal duties, they feel that they are going to non-spiritual or secular duties. Hence they do not hesitate to do wrong things. Some people feel that the spiritual life is different and it is to be lived after getting old or after retirement. This type of understanding is not proper. There are no two types of living — one spiritual and the other secular. Spirituality is understood as going to worshipping places, thinking of God, doing fasting, wearing a separate kind of dress, contributions, *bhajans*, chants and so on. People are in such notion.

All the people are holy and they have to live a holy life all the time. The holiness is to be cultivated in the mind. Holiness is not external features like wearing *dhoti*, adding some marks on face and body, fasting, and so on. Holiness is feeling divinity all the time in life within oneself and performing all actions and duties with pure mind. Knowledge of the subject is not enough, one should become a part of it. Knowledge of the medicine does not help the body. The medicine should merge into the body for healing.

For example, devotees of Ayyappa, Kanakadurga and other followers are living a particular assigned holy life, taking vow (*diksha*) for some days. Most of such devotees are living in holiness during the period of vow. They are following their vow in patience in these days and are living in holy company (*satsang*). Hence there is no possibility to them to involve in negative or unwanted activities. They are able to perform both normal duties and spiritual activities properly. This discipline and holiness is to be continued still further in their lives, even after the days of vow are completed. This is real happy and holistic living.

The real nature of human being is pure consciousness. It is the reality — the *atma*. Hence Sri Sathya Sai Baba in his discourses addresses the people as *atma svarupulara* (embodiments of *atma*) or *prema svarupulara* (embodiments of love).

We must be holy all the life in all occasions and in all our actions (*dharma karmas*). One has to feel that one is performing actions to the cause of him, as he himself is *Brahmasvarupa*. He is performing actions to the cause of his family members, as family members are *Brahmasvarupas*. In doing his actions he is associated with many people who are also *Brahmasvarupas*. All the creation is *Brahmasvarupa* (*vishvarupam*). If one performs one's actions with this thought in mind, no other type of worship is necessary. This is *jnana* and State of Equanimity.

Nowadays worship has become adorning the images by various materials. Prerecorded chantings and the hymns are repeated mechanically through electronic speakers. People feel that this is *bhakti* and devotion.

Lord Krishna's *Bhagavad-Gita* is an excellent text that teaches how to live and what to do. It has answers to all the queries and questions related to life and universe. People must follow this to live a happy and holy life. But alas! people are remembering and listening to *Bhagavad-Gita* mechanically through electronic voice speakers as a funeral text on the occasion of death.

Lord Sri Krishna, Buddha, Jesus and Mohammad symbolized what humans can become. But now what we are doing is, we adore them by adorning their images. They showed us a great path to what we can be. We are not to worship them, we are to become them or atleast follow them faithfully. This is real spiritual living.

Vedula Murthy

Contents

Introduction

THE world is full of live objects, in which human being is the most dynamic and potential. The earth is a very sacred place and human birth is a blessing. Great civilizations are flourishing in the world since long time. People are living their lives in different ways. There is continuous materialistic development everywhere. There are likes, dislikes, developments, destructions, wars and chaos in the societies. Life is a gift to be harnessed by clean thoughts. Life is a journey from womb to tomb.

Irrespective of religion, people have to live, flourish and elevate to a better plane of living. One should believe in the welfare of all without any discriminations of caste, creed, colour, sex, community or class. One has to align himself in one's thoughts, words and deeds and never think ill of others. It is not important how long one lives, but how well. Just as a horse shakes the dust that clung to its body after it rolled in sand to recoup from exhaustion of running long distances, so also one should get rid of all his negative dislikes, displeasures and sensual attractions. The riches may make life prosperous, but it is only through practice of patience, perseverance, respect towards human values, self-assessment and understanding the self, that one can make himself progressive towards peace.

The great civilization, culture and a way of nurtured and cultured life was developed in the land of Bharat (India) and is in existence since thousands of years. The life structure and life cycle was well understood and firmly described in great ancient scriptures and epics. The great knowledge acquired by the sages was taught and passed on to generations from teacher to disciples through oral chanting and repetitions. They lived as role models and strived in imparting the knowledge to the seekers. Mind is used to the full extent to the micro level.

Today people are occupied too busily in world affairs. They think worldly life is different from spiritual life. The scriptures do not advocate such division. Material and spiritual life are intertwined. Hence all actions must be holistic. Sri Ramakrishna Paramahansa showed by practice that it is not necessary to renounce worldly life to live a holy life. It is possible for a householder also to live a holy life just like most of the ancient sages who were householders.

A householder may not give up all possessions, but he can limit and moderate his desires, actions and needs. One should limit the habits of eating, dressing, owning property, etc.

People are not aware of the truth and they are living with different blind beliefs. They are not prepared to know the truth by the way they live. In order to live a happy life, one should understand the importance of life and seek to bring a change in one's approach towards life. We must have the highest ideal. Most persons live a life without having any ideal.

One has to cultivate the habits like simple living and high thinking. Some people try to imitate others often. Living originally is not properly considered in today's modern society. Imitations and repetitions are treated as fashion. You are very special and no one can play your role better than you; hence do not imitate. Live originally of your own. Then you can create something new and unique of your own.

Everyone of us has a role to fulfil, a work to do and a place, which we alone can occupy.

Everyday we hear sad and bad news of violence, wars, killings, and disasters. There is fear and tension among the people. Our precious life is not safe. We should question the progress that we made in these days of Science and Technology. Our modernity cannot replace age-old spiritual values that are responsible for peaceful progress of civilizations.

Life is not just about how much one earns and succeeds. Most people live an ordinary life of instincts and impulses like mere eating, sleeping and indulging in body pleasures. One should come out of this baser tendency. It is important to develop one's personality for happy living. This is a long process of overcoming hurdles, obstacles that come in the way of one's life. This requires patience, nurture and focus.

Religion

Religion is self-culture, and self-culture is true education. There is no difference between religion and morality. A religion must teach morals.

Moral values must be taught and its importance must be understood for the welfare of the people to lead an ideal civilized society. We are civilized well, but are losing our culture. Religion and spirituality should be able to address all the issues of life and be able to help all. Today the entire world is in need of a co-operative, humanistic and morally strong society.

Swami Vivekananda said we do not need more academic education; we need more value-based education. A person who is morally educated will be better than a person who is morally bankrupt with excellent academic qualifications. Some Universities are producing and turning out highly skilled barbarians, because a framework of values is not provided in education to teach the young people. Men are valuable than the wealth of the world, he said.

Some of the religious acts made healthy, wealthy and peaceful societies. But some people exploit the religion for their personal causes and luxuries. Fanatics are produced due to improper understanding of religion. Money is playing the role in religion and worshipping places. There are a number of religions in the world, but what is the use of these if they do not produce character-building persons? There is no separate religion outside. One's life itself is religion. One should deeply feel this and bring transformation from within. All modes of worship, work and struggle are paths for realization.

Though education and other facilities are available extensively, moral education is not imparted; hence there is degradation in moral and human values. Great civilizations were wiped out not because of any natural aggression from outside, but because of degradation of man's moral values. Even educated men become clever devils without human values. Respect for human life is decreasing. Human life is not considered precious. Wrongdoing seems no more wrong. Human beings are measured in mass and molecules, forgetting that there is a spiritual spark inherent in every human being.

Religions also have led to destruction of certain human values. There are conflicts between two sections of thoughts in the same religion or between two sections of the same society or so on. The religions divided the society into many sections not agreeing with each other.

Sometimes, we witness some people severely indulging in killing people, arson and rioting in the name of religion and God. This is highly condemnable. No religion advocates killing, slaughter and violence. Does any religion advocate this? All the religions give the same message of universal love, friendliness, tolerance towards humanity, animals and nature.

The worthiness of a society or a nation depends on the worthiness of individuals who make it. The individuals and the societies are interdependent and both should co-operate and work hand in hand.

The science is for the betterment of the humans. The moral values, which are related to every human being, are also for the betterment of humans. Both these have a common virtue and goal. Hence both science and values have to move together to achieve the common goal. You may not become a man of success, but try to become a man of values.

We must be Industrious

Work brings joy, and work gives encouragement and inspiration. The joy of work increases our energy to work. Work is the best remedy for all the ills. Those who have achieved something great have worked hard and they were wholly absorbed in their work. Such work gave them limitless joy and contentment. Thomas Alva Edison, the great genius who made more than two hundred inventions said, "Inventions are not accidents; they are the rewards for unceasing efforts." Hence we have to work hard and derive satisfaction from that work. To attain this satisfaction one must be committed to work.

We get valuable objects and products only by means of continuous efforts. Walking slowly can cover long distances. A huge construction can be built brick by brick. A little progress everyday adds to big results. Also we must perform our duties with love and affection. It is not important how much quantity of work is done, but how much quality of work is performed or produced.

A person who performs his actions with determination develops enormous spirit of self-confidence. He develops strength of mind that cannot be discouraged by failures. He gets opportunities to guide and help others. His individuality takes a definite shape for the better. Even a small progress acts as a force that leads him forward. By this, his efficiency in work goes on increasing. Because he is proficient and thorough in his work, he need not be afraid of others.

One has to learn and realize the truth that none other than himself makes his life. An individual is the in-charge of his life and has to be proactive. One has to work on his own for his growth. An individual's development is only in his hands. One should not blame others for his failures if any.

Most of the individuals act within the limit they themselves set, not being aware of their potentialities and possibilities. What a miraculous instrument our body is? What marvellous energy lies hidden within us? But we have been closing our eyes with our palms and complaining that it is dark.

We have no aspirations in our life and no specific objectives. We have no confidence in our own strength. We would not like to work according to the rules of the game. We only want to spend time in gossip. How can we ever get success? The success of our life depends on the way we live every moment, every hour and every day of our life.

Many of us work well individually. Some who are too individualistic do not like to work with others. Working alone may not suit all occasions. Hence we must learn and have to work with others. Many hands make the work light. Hence, learn to work in teams. Focus on togetherness, not on differences. No good result can be achieved without persistence and consistency.

Work done with concentration brings joy and contentment. Salary, increments and perks are not the only encouraging criteria of work and success. The attitude and efficiency in the execution of work improves standards and ensures satisfaction to the performer. Cultivate the habit of doing the task in the best possible manner. This habit increases our strength and power. Then there will be an improvement in our whole personality.

Even small bits of work also should not be neglected or ignored. Sometimes these small bits of work and trifles contribute to perfection. Do not perform your actions with insincerity. It may become a habit and it may pervade all your actions and may hamper your development.

Absence of work culture is a common complaint nowadays. Much of inefficiency and lack of enthusiasm towards work is traced. This is because of the absence of right attitude towards life and towards oneself. Great tasks are achieved not by sudden application of strength but by steady and long-drawn effort. Do not look for shortcuts. It will hamper your proper growth. Shortcuts may create short circuits in your life. If we get something free of cost or without putting our efforts, we do not find value in it. When something comes easily, we will be demanding. The result we get after putting our hard work gives much satisfaction.

In this world of severe competition some people are striving hard to get themselves fit to the hard competitive situations. And in another corner people are demanding social equality. Cry for equality may not bring justice and progress all the time. It may downgrade the society.

Commitment is the language of the wise; complaint is the language of the fools. Commitment is taking responsibility and accountability, whereas the complaint is to stay away from responsibility. If you want to lead, you should take responsibility.

People often complain that the environment in which they work is unsuitable and they are put to many external influences, which cause stress and anxiety. In general, this appears to be true. But this situation can be overcome by controlling the self and by proper practice. There is no need for us to react instantly to all the external situations. We have the choice to accept or reject while reacting to these external influences. It is not right to lay the blame on the environment or the Almighty for the injustices that we suffer in our life. We should accept life and learn to face different hard situations in life with equanimity. Flowery path may not lead to glory or progress.

We must stop judging and ill-commenting on others. Because, this promotes negative response from them. We are not aware of the factors that influence a person's state of mind. For instance, an officer may be under much pressure due to various roles that he plays in his family and social life as a husband, parent, son, friend, relative, colleague, superior, peer, subordinate or so on. All these can influence his work. Hence our judgement on others may be quite false or incomplete.

The qualities like regularity, punctuality, self-control, industriousness, sense of duty, responsibility, creativity, desire to serve, equality, fraternity, democratic attitude and sense of environmental protection are to be stressed.

Happiness

We manufacture our own unhappiness by thinking unhappy thoughts by the negative feeling that everything is going to turn out bad, or that other people are getting what they do not deserve and we are failing to get what we deserve. This attitude is to be properly self-examined and controlled by practice. Practising the habit of happy thinking simply develops happiness. Happiness is not something you find. It is something you create. True happiness comes from inner core of our being. It can never come from outside. It is the thing to be practised. Happiness and sorrow cannot be exactly spoken. They are not same to all. Another sees differently what we see as happy. Something that made us happy earlier may make us unhappy now.

The way to happiness is to follow moral values based wholly on common sense. Other ways to happiness suggested by some experts are to keep our heart free from hate and our mind free from worry. Live simply, expect little, and give much. Fill your mind with love. Do as you would like to be. If you try, you can achieve happiness by yourself. You have to like and love the people. Try to behave as per others' choice. Help them, praise them, encourage and motivate them and get their help. We should be able to say that I never met a person whom I do not like.

If people do not like you, there may be something wrong in you. Do not assume that the fault lies in them. Assume that the trouble is within you and try to find out and eliminate it. Try to give happiness to others. It is a great act of charity. This of course is very difficult and it requires honesty, simplicity and high understanding.

We want happiness and peace. But often we do not know how to get it and wherefrom to get it. And we try to seek this happiness through the use of senses. But the happiness received through the senses does not last long.

We have to find happiness in every sphere of our work. Our happiness depends on various factors mainly like our health (physical and mental), relations with our parents, spouse, children, colleagues and others, security factors like money and property, happiness in our job, habits, our future life, social status like fame, name, and interest towards our life. All these contribute together to our happiness.

Happiness and pleasure are different. Momentary happiness is pleasure. The real happiness is satisfaction. Further happiness and peace are different. Peace is above happiness. Absence of sorrow and happiness is peace. This is achieved only by fulfilling our responsible duties and following the path of *dharma*.

Freedom

Freedom is most important and is a cherished gift. Freedom is fearlessness. Without freedom one cannot develop. But this freedom should not hamper the individual or affect the society. Every one has the right to own his freedom and develop his personal growth. Consciously or otherwise, we are in continuous search for freedom from the fetters of life.

Our freedom should not discomfort others. One can enjoy freedom without curtailing the liberty of others. But the freedom should not be unconditional. More freedom simply creates indiscipline. Unconditional freedom may spoil and degrade the individual and the society. If a boundary is not established on personal freedom, one may become anti-social or sometimes a threat to the society. Freedom should not lead to recklessness. It is often better to be in chains than to be free. Only a matured person is fit to handle freedom.

When people are free to do as they please, they usually imitate and copy others. Restriction of freedom creates new innovation.

Good and Bad

Good and bad co-exist like two sides of a coin. In all the eras (*yugas*), these existed with strong roots. Rama and Ravana both lived in *Treta-yuga*. Likewise it was Sri Krishna and Kamsa, Dharmaraja and Duryodhana lived in a period of *Dvapara-yuga*. These good and evil exist in all the eras. The Sun, the Moon and the Wind are the same in all these eras. The laws of nature and the mankind are the same in all ages.

A most favourable situation to one may be unfavourable to another. The situation lies like this every where in this world. A good catching situation to a tiger is a most agonizing death to a deer.

You get the reap what you sow. If you sow paddy, you do not get millets instead. This is the law of nature. Good deeds bring good results and bad deeds bring bad results. Your today's happiness is the result of what you did yesterday (past) and your tomorrow's happiness depends on what you do today (present). Hence we should make full use of the present for tomorrow's better results.

We accuse others being wicked or bad and we settle with a kind of opinion on others. This is to be properly checked by us. Before blaming others, we must examine our weaknesses. Moreover if we search for a person who does not have any fault, we will find no one.

Remember your wrong actions will not change your life for the better. Only good deeds can bring a favourable change in your life. The God lies within everyone. If you really love God and have faith, then love all the creatures of God first. If you do not love the children of God, then how can you ever love God or anything else? Goodness or God cannot be bought with money or by religious pretence.

There is eternal conflict between good and evil. Both these divine and demonic traits are inherent in everyone. This conflict arises due to egoism and confusion regarding what is to be done and what is to be avoided. Honest self-examination can bring out both evil and good tendencies in the individual who can consciously avoid the evil and cultivate goodness. Let us be good for our own sake on our own responsibility.

Pride and Ego

Ego (*ahamkara*) is the cause of our pride. Due to this false pride we think that we are correct and others are wrong. We do not try to understand and learn from others about their useful experiences. This is due to our ego. We are associated more with our physical body and we feel this body as "I". But the real "I" in everyone is the Supreme Reality.

An individual accumulates knowledge, possessions and he settles with his image and all this builds into ego. The individual separates himself from everyone and he counts his possessions. The ego becomes strong and it is most difficult to come out of it. An egoist cannot tolerate others' ego.

Body Postures

The body postures and actions play a great role that we will be witnessing every time in our life. There are different postures like greeting with folded hands, smiling, facial expressions, expressions with eyebrows, lips, hands, legs, different sitting and standing postures, etc. In these postures, there are some disciplined ones and some others disgusting and undignified. We know the meaning of these postures. It is not necessary to talk always to express something. The feeling can be expressed well by means of body postures. Nowadays this is called body language. The deaf and dumb persons communicate with each other with these signs. As matured persons, we can use these body postures to communicate. By doing this, we can reduce the use of tongue, by which our life energy is saved and sound pollution is reduced.

Greeting with Folded Hands

The great culture of greeting others by folded hands developed in the land of Bharat. We greet each other with folded hands and we offer our respects by this. The importance of this is briefly narrated here. In a group of holy persons, if a person raises his hand to strike us, can we forget that threatening gesture? Suppose this person, who is about to strike us, becomes a friend to us later. Even then every time we see him, it is his earlier aggressive posture that comes to our mind. Contrary to this, if someone offers respects to us with folded hands will we forget his attitude of respect? Hence we should conserve and cultivate these good practices.

Greeting with folded hands is better than shaking hands so that we need not touch others. Shaking hands, hugging and kissing are not good practices, where bodies physically come in contact. This is to be avoided for health reasons. To express our love and affection saluting with hands or smiling is enough.

Concern towards Environment

People use and exploit resources. But most of them do not have awareness on environment. Even if they know they do not bother about it. The trees are cut indiscriminately reducing thick green forests. The clean air is polluted due to huge emissions from industries and brick kilns. By this pollution, the atmosphere on the earth is warming up. The ice glaciers are melting and the ecological system is deteriorating. Much water is wasted in different ways. Solid wastes are thrown in water including drain outlets, domestic and industrial.

We should improve our common sense and work for the cause of improving air and water bodies free from pollution. Cleaning the rivers and lakes is taken up sometimes. But why polluting and cleaning? We say to Ganga that your water is dirty (*ganga! tera pani maila*). Prevent rivers from being polluted. Prevention is better than cure. Open water tanks are not available in towns and cities for the birds and animals to drink. Especially in summer the birds and animals suffer from thirst for want of water. We find often some birds and animals drink dirty rain water lying on roads. They consume this water in compulsion and not with interest.

Charity

When we accumulate some possessions, it is ideal to set apart a part of it for charity. The charity should not be felt as a favour, if we give something to others. Charity should not be aimed to gain respect, name and fame. This should be done with willingness. It should not be done in compulsion with a feeling of losing something or to gain something. Jain religion emphasizes more on non-possessiveness and charity. It is said, charity is the repentance for accumulation of wealth.

If a wealthy man gives up a small part of his possessions, he is well praised, but if a poor man gives out sincerely his meagre belongings it will not be noticed or recognized.

Non-violence (*Ahimsa*)

Ahimsa means non-violence and reverence for life. This is an important trait to be practised. Jain Mahavira and Buddha have greatly contributed to this. This calls for compassion and service to living beings. There are three ways of violence — physical, verbal, and mental. Beating, killing, scolding, ill-talking, sarcasms, laughing at others, etc. come under violence. Everyone should feel responsible and practise non-violence. This should be initiated from the individual first, so that the society or the community follows and absorbs it.

1

Path of Dharma (Righteousness)

GREAT sages have realized the value of lives and preached to the people to unite and to lead a holy life following the path of *dharma* (righteousness) and peace. *Dharma* is the science of values and social ethics. It is to be upheld for the harmonious functioning of all the creatures of this world. Hence it is only by protecting the *dharma* that this world can be sustained. The religions and the faiths have come into existence to spread this message. Following the path of *dharma* is a great devotion and understanding the *dharma* is real *jnana*. Performing one's duties with perfection following the path of *dharma* is the real *karma*. One should practise worshipping of God through performance of one's duties. By this one can attain perfection. Every part of the nature follows its own *dharma*. It follows its natural norms. Sages have followed the path of *dharma* and have shown this path to the people to follow.

Values in the people are essential to build a moral society. These values are moral, social, cultural and spiritual. The values are health, cleanliness, mental hygiene, manners, ethics, appropriate social behaviour, responsibility towards duty, patience, concern towards environment, etc. These should become a part of our life. Sri Harishchandra, Sri Rama, Sri Krishna and Dharmaraja and many more others firmly followed *dharma* in spite of all odd situations.

Dharma implies adherence to moral standards and eternal values to lead a virtuous life. Being honest and truthful, refraining from greed, jealousy, anger, etc. and observing non-violence towards all are the tenets of *dharma*. These are applicable to all individuals, besides certain daily duties towards one's family and the society.

As we are living on this earth, we should follow certain universal norms or, say, elementary virtues (*samanya dharma*) like truth-speaking, non-violence, non-covetousness; purity of mind and body. An individual cannot plead ignorance of this *dharma*.

No one wants to get hurt under any circumstances. One should not hurt another. This is common sense and this is *samanya dharma*. Even an animal knows this and it avoids getting hurt. But animals cannot distinguish between right and wrong. It will protect itself from getting hurt and will not feel bad if it hurts another. But man has discrimination to distinguish between right and wrong.

The simplest way to follow *dharma* is: Do to others what you expect others to do to you, or in other words do not do to others what you do not want others to do to you.

Adhering to truth and *dharma* is very difficult for the people, especially to those in the higher ranks of power and pelf. Generally powerful people are surrounded by those who praise and boast by speaking what suits them, instead of advising them properly. One can learn from history about the persons who suffered because of listening to the counsellors who misled them.

The four principles that the people have to follow are:

1. *Dharma* — Adherence to moral values and ethical life,
2. *Artha* — Earning money for livelihood by right means,

3. *Kama* — Fulfilling desires, and
4. *Moksha* — Striving to get out of world bondage.

The pursuit of wealth or the fulfilment of worldly desires should be in accordance with *dharma,* i.e. by following proper morals and ethics. The scriptures reiterate on man's development, progress and achievement of highest excellence. They do not condemn man's pursuit of worldly wealth and power, nor do they condemn any values pursued by man. But they reiterate that there is something more valuable and higher than all these and this truth is best to be properly understood and absorbed.

Dharma is to be followed in letter and spirit at every walk of our life, i.e. in our private life, public life, administration, procedures, law, business, economics and everywhere. Here an incident from ancient texts is described.

Giving Away Old and Feeble Cows by Vajasrava — an Incident

Ceremonial gifts are generally given to the priests after performing Vedic sacrifices (*yagas*). Vajasrava, the father of Nachiketa gave away to the priests, the old and feeble cows which are of no use, to get rid of them. The son Nachiketa objected to this. The father felt angry on this and said he would give Nachiketha to Yama (the god of death).

One should not pronounce such harsh and fatal words even unintentionally. This shows the extent to which anger can distort one's sense of values. One has to give whole-heartedly what is worthy. Here Vajasrava had committed two mistakes; one is giving away unworthy gifts and the other is uttering harsh words on his son. It is better that one may not perform such dishonest rituals or one can restrict such holy worships or sacrifices. One should follow the *dharma* in letter and spirit.

Ravana and Duryodhana had all the abilities and strengths, but they did not follow the path of *dharma* and hence they perished. Vibhishana in the court of Ravana stood for *dharma* without any fear. He advised Ravana to return Sita to Rama to avert the war. Egoistic Ravana did not listen to the sane advice of Vibhishana.

Dhritarashtra and Vidura lived closely together. But their understandings and visions were different. Dhritarashtra was always disturbed, frightened and lived in tension because of selfishness and bondage of love towards his sons, while Vidura was free from all desires and was unafraid.

One should develop self-control and patience and eliminate hatred towards others. Performing duties according to one's position (*svadharma*) is essential to stay tuned to *dharma* and it is the real holistic living. To earn money and to fulfil our desires we work hard. But when it comes to fulfilling duties or doing noble actions we do not like to come forward. To escape from such actions we say that past *karma*s or the God will take care of us. This is not proper.

In these days as the ways of livelihood are changed, hence some people confuse and question the matters like values, following *dharma* and on how to take ideal decisions in certain matters. One should not feel that *dharma* is an old concept followed in ancient times and is outdated to present-day living. Righteousness is essential all the time to upkeep the individuals and the society. Here it is to say that there are no hard and fast rules or absolute or instant solutions to follow immediately. One has to understand the situation and use discrimination and take proper decision to follow.

The actions to be followed in one's life as per the age are prescribed in some scriptures as follows.

- In childhood it is all learning and education.

- In youth, the activities related to livelihood, learning through life experiences, enjoying in conformity to *dharma*.
- In old age, the activities of maturity and elevation like service, working to achieve the goal what one is capable of gaining, doing meditation, detachment to material life are advised. This is contemplating, investigation, growing from within, practising silence and so on.
- And the last is learning and practising to leave the body in health through *yoga*.

Following these activities is a social value system. If everyone follows this, a separate governance or an anarchy may not be necessary or it may be for namesake only.

2

Control of Senses

THE senses are the powerful bodily faculties by which sensation and instinct are roused. These are the eyes, ears, nose, tongue and the skin. These are different wonderful organs in the body to see, hear, smell, taste and touch. These senses are very much necessary and are to be used to sustain the body. The senses react very actively and want to satisfy their desires with the help of mind. In fact, a desire rises in the mind and the mind excites the sense organs.

Human being has got all the advantages over other creatures of the world. But he has equal disadvantage of having highly active senses. Other creatures act according to their natural basic instincts like eating, mating and self-defence.

Some animals are well attracted by their active sense instinct as follows:

- A deer is attracted to the sound and is caught by the sweet voice of the flute.
- A fish is attracted to the food.
- A black bee gets attracted by the perfume of *champaka* flower.
- An elephant is tempted by the touch of a female elephant and is trapped.
- A moth gets lured to the fire flame and dies.

These creatures meet their end as a consequence of falling prey to the sensory attraction.

These creatures had only one active sense and what to say of a human, who had five active senses. He becomes slave to all the five senses that pull him in different directions. Man incurs sins sidetracked by these senses and may fail to discharge his obligatory duties. Hence one should take care of these aspects and develop control over the senses by controlling his mind. The senses cannot act on their own without the help of the mind. Mind wishes, desires and stimulates the sense organs to act what it intended or desired.

The great Ravana performed severe penance with perfect control and secured invincible powers as a boon. But later he became a victim to his own senses, when he longed for Sita. The senses are powerful and they distract the individuals from pursuing their goals.

Sri Ramakrishna Paramahamsa often stressed to be cautious of two types of desires. They are sensory attractions (material) and next the subtle ones like yearning for name and fame. Majority of people are attracted and strive for these often.

If the mind runs along the senses then the problem aggravates and the individual may have to suffer in life due to the indiscriminate use of senses. The use of senses is to be controlled by controlling the mind and by the use of intellect (*buddhi*) and discrimination (*vivekam*).

Mastery over sense organs and their moderate indulgence is very essential. Freedom is not produced by full enjoyment of what is desired but is achieved by controlling the desires.

Desires arise one after another in everyone. It is natural for each sense organ to feel attraction or aversion in respect of objects. The sensory attractions (*raga*) and aversions (*dvesha*) build pressure in the mind. Unless these are neutralized an individual cannot keep calm.

A big pot full of water can be emptied by a small hole. Even a little anger or ego will burn all the nobility earned since long years of practice.

One gets peace of mind by disciplining the senses. But this is not that easy as said. Because by nature senses are active, outward bound and they run towards attractions. Only by conscious, rigorous and sincere practice one gets control over the senses.

There is difference between pleasure achieved by the senses and the happiness of the heart. Happiness is not pleasure, it is intrinsic. Controlling the senses is made possible only by the mind. When the mind desires something, it should think, analyse and discriminate before it orders the organs. Hence the mind is to be kept controlled by different practices, so that it can govern well the senses.

There are large numbers of temptations everywhere. Some of them are natural and some are man-made. Here a small story is narrated on how the temptations influence the people.

Successor to a King — A Story

A king wanted to choose an ideal, able and determined successor after his retirement. He wanted his successor to be a person with strong will-power, who is not tempted by ordinary joys, pleasures, material desires and so on, because a king has to deal with the people's problems wisely in a justified manner without being lured by temptations.

For this purpose, the king arranged a critical test for the aspirants. The aspirants have to go through this test. The king arranged a big exhibition of various materials, dances, songs, food, etc. The exhibition is made with dazzling and glamorous scenes with many tempting materials. The aspirants can take or use anything free of cost. They can eat, drink, bathe, swim, play, fight, sing, dance and enjoy anything they want. There is no need to pay for anything that he wished to have or enjoy. All the aspirants must pass through this exhibition to reach the king's palace where the aspirant has to meet the king at a scheduled time.

Many young candidates passed through this exhibition to become the successor to the king. But all of them got stuck by temptation at one or other point and they could not reach the king in time. Some of them have forgotten their very purpose of visiting the exhibition and became slaves to the pleasures and failed. They could not control their mind and senses.

But one determined and mentally stable man had passed through this exhibition, reached and met the king at the appointed time. The king felt very happy to see his successor, who withstood the test with courage and determination without being tempted by the mundane pleasures.

The story tells that there are large numbers of endless temptations in this world. If one has a goal to reach, one has to let go and sacrifice all the temptations on the way to realize the goal.

Keeping control over the senses and the mind is the greatest virtue in one's life.

3

Food that we Eat

WE are what we eat. Tell me what you eat and I will tell you what you are, says an expert. Man is what he eats. Our health depends on the food that we eat and on the habits that we practise.

The basic need for all the creatures to live is the food, i.e. some substance to be supplied to the stomach. It digests in the stomach and mixes in the blood. Food is the fuel to the body, without which the body cannot sustain or live. Every creature tastes and eats food what the nature has set for it. Some creatures take vegetarian leaf and plant materials as food and some others take non-vegetarian flesh food. Non-vegetarian eating animals are predators and they prey on other animals. The animals consume uncooked natural food as per their natural tendency.

The food of the human beings is different. Before civilization, man used to take natural food like fruits, roots and leaves. After seeing the animals prey on other animals, he started killing some animals and used to consume raw flesh.

During the course of time, civilizations developed. Man started consuming cooked food of agricultural products. From then the variety of food multiplied into large numbers of cuisines with different new tastes. Now the taste became a matter of importance than its content and nutrition.

Though varieties of tastes are available, man is not satisfied and he is searching for new tastes. Man consumes both vegetarian and non-vegetarian food.

As per the law of nature humans have to consume natural food only, without its cooking or boiling. But the man calling himself civilized is consuming cooked food after getting the food ingredients go through long process in boiling and cooking. Anyway the cooked food must be accepted and should not be denied in these days of civilization and a binding system of society.

An important point to be noted is that the food must be simple, nutritious and healthy. Tasty food and healthy food are different. All the tasty foods may not be healthy. Our food should be simple, tasty and economical and should keep our health. Unnecessary addition of too many ingredients and spices to add taste and smell should be avoided in making cooked food items, as the addition of spices and extra boiling reduces the nutritious values of food.

The teeth structures of vegetable eating animals and flesh eating animals are made different to allow them to facilitate their eating easy and convenient. Water drinking style of these animals also is different. The teeth structure of humans matches to the teeth of leaf eating animals. Man's teeth are normal, simple and are made to eat vegetable food only. Moreover vegetable food is healthy and nourishing. Hence animal food is discouraged. Our body is sustaining only on the food that we take. So, the effect of food is there not only on our body, but it affects our brain and our thoughts also. Generally it seems ridiculous that the food affects our thoughts, but it is true whether it is believed or not.

Our body should be nourished with pure food which gives strength, health and cheerfulness. It also needs pure fresh air. We must avoid intoxicants, stimulants and drugs.

The food that we take and the people may be divided into three types. This is well explained by Lord Krishna in the seventeenth chapter of *Bhagavad-Gita*.

Tamas

The stale food cooked long time back, spoiled food, the food preserved in refrigerators, alcohols, intoxicants, all come under this category. This food is not advisable to consume as it makes the consumer dull, lazy and sleepy. It spoils the health and the mind. The dull (*tamas*) category people prefer this and they consume such stale food and intoxicants.

> *yata-yamam gatarasam puti paryushitam cha yat* ।
> *ucchishtam api chamedhyam bhojanam tamasa-priyam* ॥
>
> Half baked, juiceless, bad smelling, stale and foul food is liked by the people of *tamas* nature.
>
> —*Bhagavad-Gita*, 17.10

Rajas

The other category is too hot and too cold food. The boiling food just brought from the hot pan should not be consumed immediately as a fashion. Too hot drinks and too cold drinks are to be avoided. Excess sugar, sweets, hot chilly, sours and spicy (*masala*) food are not advisable to consume. The persons who actively work (*rajas*) prefer this food. But this food also may possibly spoil the health and it affects the thoughts and the brain.

> *katvamla-lavana-athyushna tikshna-ruksha-vidahinah* ।
> *ahara rajasasyeshta duhkha-shoka mayapradah* ॥
>
> Bitter, sour, salty, chilly, excess hot and fried foods, sad and ill causing food is consumed by the people of *rajas* nature.
>
> — *Bhagavad-Gita*, 17.9

Sattva

The last category of food is simple, clean and normal, not too cold, not too hot, not sour, not too sweet and not too chilly. The food is moderate in all aspects. The people with moderate temperament (*sattva*) consume this food. Moderate food keeps the mind not only moderate, but it keeps the mind more active and non-sleepy. Their mind is stable and they can work for long hours without feeling dullness and stress.

The food served in brahmins' houses, temples and *ashrams* consists of some of the following useful simple and tasty items: rice, fresh vegetables, pulses, wheat, nuts, milk, butter, ghee, etc. cooked to their normal taste. In addition to this fruits are also consumed.

> *ayuh-sattva-bala-arogya sukha-priti-vivardhanah* ।
> *rasyah snigdhah sthira hridya aharah sattvika-priyah* ।
>
> Plain and simple, strong, healthy, happy, pleasing, milk, sugar and juicy food, butter, ghee and life giving vital food is liked by the people of *sattva* nature.
>
> — *Bhagavad-Gita*, 17.8

Some people eat food indiscriminately at any time. We take food to live, but not live to eat food. The food should be taken at a scheduled time and more water is to be consumed. We love our body and hence strict regimen is to be made for its health and control. Nothing can be healthier than pure fresh water. Consuming more fresh water heals many ills and it keeps health well. Intoxicants are strictly prohibited. The stomach should be filled with food only up to 60 per cent of its capacity and the remaining is left for water and empty space. Eat moderately and drink more water during the day. Vegetables, leaf, fibre food and fruits are better food. Fats, oils, and fried food are to be reduced and avoided.

Nowadays people are wasting food, especially in hotels. It has become a fashion to eat in hotels and wasting precious food carelessly. Food should not be wasted at all. There are countless people in this world who are starving or not able to have minimum food or not having nutritious food suffering malnutrition or death. Everything came from Reality (God), so also food. We can live without other materials, but we cannot live without food.

Hence it is said, *annam parabrahma svarupam*. Hence food is sacred and holy. The food is to be offered first to the Supreme Reality and then to be eaten. The offered food becomes holy, sacred and becomes *prasad*.

Our eating and the food should be in complete discipline. It should be such that the food itself should be a medicine to our body. By consuming such food, we are away from the ills and need not use medicines at all. But nowadays most people are using stomach as dustbin and they are pushing junk food indiscriminately into stomach through mouth and are suffering from its ill effects and are going to doctors for treatment. Prevention is better than cure. Hence we must change our food habits to keep fit our health, wealth and mind.

Fasting on Occasions

There are different views and versions on fasting. Fasting makes a person acquire self-control, develop strong will power, bring passions under control and helps economy and food saving. The persons on fasting day are not dull and instead they are active and vigorous. Water and other soft liquid food can be taken during fasting. The fasting reduces fat and keeps body lighter. Sometimes scarcity of food and famine are to be faced. In the time of famine, if the people restrict consumption of food to one time daily, the available food can be served for double period of time.

4

Spiritual Knowledge

SPIRIT is the soul or life, which is the essence by which all the creatures are living in this universe. If this spirit is missing in a body, it is useless, lifeless and becomes filthy. Christ said, "what is the use of having the whole world and loses his own soul?" Man is the spirit enveloped in matter. Only human being is aware of the knowledge of spirit and its importance.

In this connection an interesting story is explained here to emphasize the importance of spiritual knowledge and holiness.

Greatness of Animals — A Story

Once upon a time an intelligent fox started thinking seriously comparing the greatness of animals with that of the humans. The fox felt that man is after all a small personality, who does not have any muscle power or teeth strength or running capacity when compared to many animals. It felt that a human being is weak in all aspects, and animals are stronger than humans. Hence it wanted to convey this message to all other animals. It wants to convene a meeting of all animals to discuss and want to show the power of animals.

The fox went to the elephants and said, "O, Elephants! You are very large in size and heavy; you possess great strength and power. No man can equal you in strength and size." And the fox invited all the elephants to attend the scheduled "Great Animals meet" without fail.

The fox also met the lions and tigers and said, "you are strong, your teeth are too sharp, you are the fastest runners and no man equals you in any of your capabilities." And it invited the lions and tigers to the scheduled "Great Animals meet." Likewise, it met the buffaloes, horses, camels, dogs, giraffes, other animals, snakes and birds and explained the matter and requested all the animals to attend the animals' meeting scheduled at a particular place in the forest.

Then the fox had formed a core committee consisting of some important animals to discuss the issues of the animals' meet. Other animals expressed that as the meeting is arranged to show the power of the animals, hence a man must be present in the meeting. Then the fox got an idea and said, "there is a sage (*rishi*) living in the forest, he is weak and does not possess any strength when compared to all of us. He is better for this meeting; we will call him as guest of the animals' meet." Other animals accepted this proposal.

Then the fox went to the sage and explained the idea of convening animals' meet and invited him as chief guest. The sage accepted the invitation.

Oh! The day of the meeting has arrived. The animals are very happy and they have attended the meeting in large numbers at the venue. They are making their own sounds and are cheerful. The venue is all filled with the sounds of animals like gibbering of apes, braying of asses, humming of bees, chirping of birds, bleating of calves, barking of dogs, trumpets of elephants, yells of fox, bleats of goats, neighs of horses, roars of lions, speaks of parrots, hisses of snakes, chatters of monkeys, grunting of camels, and so on.

Some of the animals were gossiping like this, "we all animals are here, the chief guest is a lean man, he may get frightened, I doubt whether he comes to this meeting or not."

Then it is exactly the time of the meeting and the sage who is the chief guest of the "Great Animals Meet" arrived. The meeting started. The fox has invited the important animal speakers and also the chief guest to the dais.

The fox started the meeting and in her opening address, it has narrated the physical size and strength of animals in detail. It has explained the strength of elephants and lions, the teeth strength of tigers and crocodiles, the speed of tigers and horses, power of the snakes, flying capacity of birds and so on. Likewise other animals also have apprised their strengths. All the animals pointed out that human being is weak when compared to animals. They have questioned the greatness of humans. All the participant animals are in cheers and enjoying the meeting well.

After the completion of the speeches of all animals on the dais, the fox invited the sage to address the gathering. The sage in his address has applauded all the animals and accepted that the animals are powerful than human beings. Then there are cheers, claps and shouting among the animals.

Further the *rishi* continued that the special unique power a human being possesses is spiritual knowledge. It is concerned to non-matter. It is holy, divine, sacred, soul, supernatural and spirit. Suddenly there is silence in the meeting. The animals are not able to understand the words. The *rishi* concluded his address saying that the difference between animals and the human being is that a man possesses the spiritual knowledge and the animals do not have it. Then there is some irksomeness and uneasy calm in the animal crowd, as they do not understand this spiritual knowledge.

The fox asked the *rishi*, whether all the humans possess this spiritual knowledge. The *rishi* made it clear that not all the humans possess this knowledge, only some have it. The fox then asked the *rishi*, "could we include those humans who do not have this spiritual knowledge in our community?" The *rishi* said, yes.

Oh! There was great applauding from the animals and the silence was broken. The fox thanked the *rishi* and concluded the meeting by declaring that the human beings who possess the spiritual knowledge are honourable and further declared that the men who do not have this knowledge are all added into the large animal fraternity.

The story tells that the human being has distinct advantage over all other living beings, as man can strive towards spirituality. A human can become what he wants, what animals cannot do. The sacred birth as a human being may become waste, if it is not properly utilized.

What makes human beings different from animals is the reasoning ability and rationality. Also human beings are capable of making self-sacrifice. They can be kind and unselfish. This unselfishness is Godliness, said Swami Vivekananda. Spiritual knowledge alone gives positive outlook on life.

> *ahar nidra bhay maithunam cha samanya etat pasubhir naranam* I
> *buddhirhi thesham adhiko visesha buddhya vihinaha pasubhir samanaha* II

> Eating, sleeping, fear and procreation are common to both animal and man. The intellect distinguishes man from animal. Without this intellectual character man is same as animal.

The spiritual knowledge consists of the knowledge of birth, existence and death of creatures, the functioning of bodies, living a holy life, state of equanimity, the sustaining energy of this universe and so on. Some of these are explained in the next chapters.

5

Divine life

DIVINE life means to live a holy and sacred life. The divinity in other terms is called spirit. It is the soul and life, which is the vital essence in the universe. Living a holy life should not be misunderstood that it is meant for certain extraordinary men with special qualifications. Spiritual life is not to live in thick forests or in some lonely area. It is not achieved suddenly by running away from our occupations or by living an idle beggarly life in some remote hills or a valley. The votary of divine life need not change his clothes or add some marks on his forehead and body or stand upon head for some hours in the sun or keep long hair (*jata*) or shave the head or sit on a bed of nails or meditate on tiger's skin. Mere wearing of a particular colour dress or ochre robes does not make a devotee or a Sanyasi. These external shows are not necessary to a real devotee.

Spiritual life is not dependent on the place where you live or the clothes you wear, or the condition of your hair or the beard. It is neither connected with the vessels you use nor the bed you sleep on. This divinity does not have any connection with man-made divisions like religion, caste, colour, creed, language, gender and so on.

Spiritual life is not reciting *mantras*, visiting temples and worshipping deities, etc. It is something that we have to evolve from within. This is to be achieved by living a divine life. It is a systematic and disciplined way of living with certain noble values.

Everyone is divine and the whole universe is divine. Hence one can be free, happy and holy irrespective of one's conditions like rich or poor, sick or healthy, educated or uneducated and so on.

We bathe our physical body, we clean it with soaps and shampoos, we scent it, powder it and beautify it. But we do not have patience and time to attend to the filthy condition of our inner personality. And we know that our inner character is important and essential. But mostly we neglect it. We always think that something else is necessary to make us happy. This is the reason why people go after things that they think will make them happy. If you want happiness and peace, make your happiness by building the conditions necessary.

It is often questioned and thought as to which of the spiritual practices are superior to perform. This is due to the tendency in the individual to choose the best when given a choice. Here to lead a divine life different practices and cults like *bhakti, karma* and *jnana* are prescribed to the seekers who can select and practise depending on their capacity of understanding, experience and environment.

Lord Krishna stated that actions are to be performed with no attachment to its results. They should be performed with an attitude of submission to the Reality. Such actions purify the mind, and then mind becomes eligible and elevates to the next higher levels. This transforms into *yoga*. *Yoga* means union, i.e. union of the selfless pure mind with the Reality, the *atma*.

Devotional Cult-worship (Bhakti)

Devotion indicates pure love, affection and surrender. It is a pure state of mind, where there is no scope for any doubt. It is like mother's keeping watch over her child, while performing her routine activities. Real devotion does not aspire anything in return. It is one-sided and is full of love.

Worshipping

Worshipping means paying reverence. It is *upasana* or *vandana*. Here some questions arise. What is worshipping? Why should it be done? Since time immemorial man is searching for happiness and he wants to find out the real sustaining potential (the Reality) of this universe and he wants to pay obeisance to that Great Reality, which is the cause of this universe and which is subtle, unseen and making this universe alive, functioning, moving and ever changing. People treat and laud this Reality in the name of God in different ways. There are nine modes of worship:

Listening	-	*shravana*
Praising	-	*kirtana*
Remembering	-	*smarana*
Worshipping	-	*archana*
Salutations	-	*vandana*
Serving	-	*daasya*
Friendship	-	*sakhyam*
Self-submission	-	*atma nivedanam*
Service to feet	-	*paad sevanam*

The few examples of votaries, who loved, praised, merged and dissolved into Reality are Ramadas, Annamacharya, Tyagaraja, Meerabai, Jayadev, etc. Meerabai loved Lord Sri Krishna as her husband and dedicated her life in singing and praising Lord Krishna without any second thought.

Meditation on the Absolute Reality is the direct means of true worship. It is Nirguna Upasana (performance to a nonform). For those who find this difficult, meditation on the Absolute with a form is recommended. Here a devotee can imagine a form of his choice and can meditate on it. Many find this also hard to pursue. Because a formless Absolute cannot be imagined in an abstract form. Hence for them worship of a representation like an image or a picture or an idol becomes necessary for the mind to develop concentration and peace. It is easy for the mind to grasp the form. The Reality is imagined, elaborated and assumed shapes into deities and are worshipped. It is elaborated into rituals. This is Saguna Upasana (Performance to a form). Different practices are adopted by different seekers. The devotion developed into following practices like:

- Worshipping images,
- Recitation of hymns,
- Visiting pilgrim places.

In other words, these may be termed as *kayika* (physical), *vachika* (oral) and *manasika* (mental). Rituals and ceremonies are *kayika*. Recitation of hymns, *bhajans*, chanting *mantras* are *vachika*. Meditation (*dhyana*) is silent and is *manasika*. In this, each one is superior to the preceding.

Worshipping Images

In this worship, the Reality is honoured as a guest and whatever one would do by way of expressing one's hospitality to a guest is offered. The sixteen-service worship (*shodashopachara puja*) corresponding to welcoming the lord, offering a seat and entertaining Lord with a feast is done in this worship. The following sixteen services are offered to the Lord.

1. Welcome - *avahan*
2. Throne of gems - *ratna-simhasan*

3.	Water to wash feet, water to wash hands	-	*padya, arghya*
4.	Sipping water (This is not the exact word in English. It is the act of sipping water taken in right hand palm three times.)	-	*achaman*
5.	Bathing	-	*snan*
6.	Clothes	-	*vastra*
7.	Sacred thread	-	*yajnopavit*
8.	Sweet water	-	*madhuparka*
9.	Sandal paste, jewels, turmeric rice, garland	-	*gandha, abharana, akshata, pushpamala*
10.	Adoring	-	*puja*
11.	Incense sticks, lighting	-	*dhup, dipa*
12.	Sacred feast, betel leaves	-	*naivedya, tambul*
13.	Camphor flame	-	*nirajan*
14.	Appraisal of God form and offering flowers	-	*mantra pushpa*
15.	Ambulation, prostrations	-	*pradakshina, sashtanga namaskar*
16.	Services like umbrella, fanning, dancing, singing and procession	-	*upachar*

At the end of this worship, the worshipper offers apologies (*kshamapana*) to God for any mistakes committed in doing this worship.

Rituals like *yajna* are also performed to please demigods.

Nowadays this ritualistic worship is treated as *bhakti*. In the temples, idol worship (*saguna aradhana*) is in practice. People follow this type of worship and they throng the temples. The idols in Indian temples are symbolic. They convey this message to the devotee, "Fear not, Trust me, I am with you, your desires will be fulfilled." Worshipping of images is very preliminary. One should come out of this and practise to see the God in all the creatures of the world.

The Supreme Reality is called by the word "God" by the people. The moment we hear the word God, we get a feeling that God is a powerful super human living somewhere in heaven far away from earth. We feel that He showers His blessings on some and punishes the sinners and so on. As we have the physical body we feel that God also has a body with head, legs, hands, etc. We apply our negative attributes also to God. As we feel angry, we feel that God also feels angry sometimes and punishes the ill-doers. This type of understanding, imagination and interpretation of God is very low and not proper. The word God itself leads to a physical form. Some assumed and perceived the Reality in different forms, and artists painted and sculpted images. God is to be understood as an Absolute Reality. People call the Reality by different names like Lord, Supreme, *Bhagavan*, *Atma*, *Brahman*, *Ishvara*, Almighty, Supreme Potential, Pure Consciousness and so on. By whatever name it is called, it is the cosmic power and does not have any form and name.

Bhakti or devotion requires application, purity and concentration of mind, without which the performances and the rituals do not mean anything and do not elevate the mind of the performer. If one worships sincerely, he becomes accomplished and gets into higher levels of mental status. It should be understood that the worship of the Lord is not merely visiting places of worship. Everything in the creation is emanated from the Reality and hence all this is pervaded by the Reality.

Performing the rituals or ceremonies in the temples is treated as *bhakti*. But their mechanical performance is pitiable. This *bhakti* is exhibited with some adoration of images, displays, assembly of some materials and offerings. All this is done with an intention of something to get in return. The emphasis on rituals made the people more interested in ritualistic actions. They undertake the performance of these with dedication and interest. These are performed to satisfy their general desires for health, wealth and other material benefits. If these are done mechanically, it may not bring any transformation in the doer. This is *muda bhakti*, which is advocated to the people of lower ranks.

It is painful to see that huge quantity of material and money is being used in spiritual and religious activities. This expenditure can be reduced and it can be used for other useful purposes if it is properly perceived and planned. Shankaracharya urged to go beyond the rituals and seek the *jnana* of ultimate truth.

By visualizing Absolute Reality in an image, the devotion is limited to a small form and only to images. Hence due to lack of proper understanding a devotee may fall to restrict his devotion only to images. By this practice a devotee may get attached to the images and may get inspired only by such images. He may not adjust and understand other faiths or other people and the world properly. This type of devotion becomes superstitious and it may not help to elevate the performer. Unless one is pure in body and mind, his going to a temple and worshipping may not fetch any benefit. True *bhakti* is seeing God outside worshipping places, temples and beyond religious ceremonies.

Swami Vivekananda said, it is in the pure and sincere love in the heart that religion exists and not in ceremony.

He urged people to worship the Lord not in images but in the poor, in the weak and in the diseased.

To call themselves as God-loving, some people use the word God-fearing. This is absurd and it is utter misunderstanding. One should not fear God. God is not fearful and does not do any harm. It is the people who cause harm. One should eliminate fear and love God. Some of the religions insist and preach often on the sins. This creates misconception and fear among the followers. Some preachers are not aware of the knowledge of God and are misguiding the people. This is happening because people imagine God as a super powerful man with automatic weapons and mysterious powers and who satisfies the desires of the people and punishes the sinners. Unless this conception is removed, one cannot understand the reality of this universe.

It is not the name of the god or the religion that elevates a person, but it is the real belief of the self that does something. To whatever religion a person may belong, one should develop unshakable faith and affirmation in himself and stick on to high discipline. Faith or disbelief is a matter of individual choice. It is the faith that makes us honest and humble. What stands between us and the Reality is our mind. Worshipping all the thirty-three crore gods mentioned in the scriptures is futile, if one does not have trust and faith in himself.

Recitation of Hymns

The universe is full of names. Every part of the Universe is named. Hence the universe can be seen in physical form and also can be heard in names. Hence it is said, *naamam idam jagat*.

The Reality is lauded, praised and worshipped by recitation of names. The name gives the form to the mind.

The worship is performed by chanting the names and verses. The *mantra* is repeated silently in this worship. But the possibility in this worship is that the seeker may habitually chant the hymns only by lips and not by heart. He may not rise to a level higher than this. We see many people who recite the hymns well in Sanskrit language. But their meaning and the real essence are not known to most of them. Just they recite the hymns and live a life in temples and missionaries (*pitha*s). The supreme Reality is beyond words and speech. It is not possible to describe it in words. In hymns a devotee restricts the glory of the Reality in finite words.

While reciting the hymns, it may become a mechanical habit of reciting. By this mechanical repetition, mind may not stay on the recitation and it goes on to other thoughts. The mind will not be attentive on the recitation, as the chanting is learned by rote. The recitor may not know their meaning also.

In early days, when human beings were not there on earth, there were no names and divisions. Before the beginning of the language there were no names. But at that time also the whole universe existed and the potential behind the universe existed. Gravitational force of the earth exists even before it is recognized. Hence the names created by man do not have connection with the reality. Names are created later for the sake of communication and convenience. Nothing is added to the universe or to the Reality by naming Its parts. On the other hand, innumerable names and divisions may create confusion. We have segregated ourselves by these divisions from the totality and hence feel limited and restricted. The material world seems to be too diversified. But if we refer to the sustaining potential behind this world, i.e. the Reality, It is only one. It is Advaita, meaning without a second one. Hence one should meditate on this one Reality.

Pilgrim Places and Temples

In India, these places are panoramic and natural often connected with mountains, valleys and rivers. Temples and shrines were built at these places. These places are considered as sacred and it is believed that the God resides here. Visiting these places is believed to be a must in one's life. Some of these places are connected to the birthplace of great spiritual personalities, or they may be the places of penance, or so on. People visit these places with belief and enthusiasm. They enjoy the sanctity and peace at these places.

All nature and its manifestations are treated as sacred and people worship them. The bodies are made with five basic elements like earth, water, fire, air and ether and hence these elements are worshipped. Great numbers of people are associated and are living in these pilgrim places and temples. People have to live their lives by some means. Hence here we can consider the analogy of "live and let live."

People visit pilgrim places often. In this visit they see and enjoy the nature, beauty, people, variety, cultures, languages and habits. They gain knowledge and experience from these visits. Also it is a fact that everyone who visits the sacred shrines is not necessarily able to behold the divine presence of the Lord in the deity. Most pilgrim places are visited as tourist spots.

In fact, the holiness is not restricted to pilgrim places alone, as the whole universe is sacred, holy and divine. It is *poornam* (full). Nothing can be removed from it. There is no holiness or unholiness in this universe. There is no such division; we impose such limitations and divisions on our own. We are unable to see everything as divine. We see many people who wear external religious appearance. But when it comes to the help or co-operation they do not come forward. Then what is the use of appearance, when there is no inner vision, ideology and understanding?

Work or Service (Karma-Yoga)

Performing one's own duty (*karma*) is believed to be a superior type of worship. Here it is asserted that if one does one's duties with sincerity and to the best of his ability, it is enough and it is the true righteousness. This gives an opportunity to interact with others, give vent to emotions and desires, when one is engaged in daily activities. This exposure helps one to acquire the skill to deal equally with joy and pain, friend and foe, success and failure, likes and dislikes, etc. This experience in turn matures and purifies the mind. Mind develops the ability to maintain equanimity. Such a stable mind is necessary to live a holistic life.

One cannot escape from work and must perform the duties all the life till one dies. Hence it is better to develop an attitude of performing the duties well with perfection and equanimity of mind.

Lord Krishna stresses more on the practice of one's ordained duties (*karma*) in a dispassionate manner with no expectation of reward. The reward goes to the performer automatically as per the performer's eligibility.

Karma is action. We perform countless actions throughout our life. If these actions are performed with commitment and with a feeling of responsibility, it creates a way and it elevates the mind. Performing one's duties is equivalent to worshipping the Reality. Therefore it is said, "work is worship." Hence one should perform the duties sincerely and affectionately without demanding the rights. Such persons rise mentally. But contrary to this, nowadays, most people fight for the cause of their rights without performing their duties.

Both *bhakti* and *karma* are necessary to live a holy life. Imagine if out of two persons one constantly sings God's praises without doing his duty, while the other does his duties quietly without chanting aloud any hymns. Then whom do we like? Obviously we like the one who does his duties. If one merely sings God's praises, without doing his normal duties, he may not be liked.

We should understand that service to people is service to God. Hence we should serve the needy people. Service means contribution. It is contribution of service, money, materials, intelligence and so on. By doing service our ego and attachments are slowly reduced.

Jnana

As was already stated, the seekers can choose different practices depending on their level of understanding and mental status. One with higher knowledge, patience and high endurance lives in a moderate state of mind. He will not be perturbed by day-to-day happenings. He adjusts to the circumstances and lives comfortably with whatever is available. Even if he lives in luxury, he does not have the desire or inclination to enjoy those comforts. His eating, talking, and sleeping are moderate.

Jnana is a mental state in which there are no desires. His senses and mind are completely under his control. Such person is called *jnani* or *sthitaprajna*. Jnani performs his duties and responsibilities with total submission to Reality and does not aspire for the result of actions. He does not fear for anything and he enjoys freedom. He is static in mind and actions. All his actions are moderate and stable.

Self-discipline

This is a greater possession than the possession of material wealth. This enables us to organize and unite all our scattered forces. This necessarily increases our power for both thought and action. A man may use high-sounding words expressing moral values, but if he lacks in fundamental principles of life like patience, forbearance, forgiveness, he may burst out sometimes in anger and may fail in keeping himself contented. A man must be able to live independently of his own. A person of self-discipline depends on his inward strength.

Anger, grief and hatred are our own enemies. It we do not control them, we have to face the consequences. Anger is one letter short of danger. He is indeed a happy man who can withstand the impulse of greed, lust and anger. Endurance is one of the great assets in life. We must exercise conscious control in our daily normal activities like eating, drinking, talking, walking, sleeping and also in our work and recreation. This enables us to gather our body forces which are now being dissipated through lack of proper control and direction to unite into one strong whole. If one patiently practises this, he can be calm, simple, ideal, successful and dynamic. It is not strong muscles that make a man stronger, but a man who governs his appetites, who lives in moderation, and who has the power to forgive is the stronger man. Self-control tends to produce a mighty will, which may make great persons like Buddha or others.

Offering Thanks to God

Everything is a part of the Reality and whatever we get is a gift from that Reality, be it food, water, shelter, education, employment, riches or health. Whatever we get, we must take it for granted that it is a gift from God. Hence we must thank for all the boons we get. It may be anything like food, money, increments, incentives, awards, rewards, honours, praise or any other material possessions small or big, we must convey our happiness and holy thanks to the Lord.

Dedicate the Results of Actions to God Everyday

Surrender all actions performed to the Almighty with faith and practise what one's religion teaches. Attending the discourses of great persons is not just to hear or to spend some time, but it is to practise the hearings and to emulate.

Cultivate the good habit of dedicating the results of actions to God everyday. When you go to sleep, remember the Reality, call the Reality, talk to the Reality through this prayer. Prayer is an effective way of coping with stress and sufferings. It is a direct act of talking to God.

NIGHT PRAYER

> O, God! Today is a good, pleasant and a peaceful day. It is spent well. Everything went on well. My thanks are to you. If I commit any mistakes in my actions or if I did any wrong actions today please forgive me. I thank and dedicate the results and fruits of all my actions of today to you. All the results of my actions are dedicated to you and there is no result of any action in me. I am pure and calm. I am now going to sleep. Please permit me to sleep. I wish that all this night passes very peacefully to me and to all. Let the peace prevail everywhere.
>
> Let all the people be happy (*sarve janah sukhino bhavantu*)
>
> Let all the worlds be happy (*samasthan lokan sukhino bhavantu*)
>
> Om, peace, peace, peace (*om, shantih, shantih, shantih*)

After this prayer of thanks and dedication of actions to the God then you sleep. When you get up from sleep early in the morning, remember and talk to God like this.

MORNING PRAYER

> O, God! I had a pleasant sleep last night. My thanks are to you. If I did any mistakes in the night, please pardon me. I dedicate the result of all my actions of last night to you. There are no more results of my actions in me at all. I am now going to perform my routine duties, hence please permit me and bless me that everything goes on well peacefully today to me and to all.

After this prayer you go to perform your day duties. Like this, one must offer sincere thanks and prayers and dedicate the fruits of actions to the Reality. By doing this, the mind gets purified slowly. And as we are in the discipline of dedicating the actions daily to God, we do not incline to commit wrong actions, because we do not want to dedicate wrong actions to God. This is the real and best way of worshipping God. This is the path of *jnana* and a divine life.

6

Interpersonal Relations

EVERYONE has an inherent desire to progress and to expand his personality. "Expansion is life and contraction is death" said Swami Vivekananda. No man is an island. We are all interdependent. We are living in an increasingly interdependent world. This dependency is seen in numerous relationships throughout our life. Building healthy interpersonal relations is difficult but very essential to live a happy life. The need to nurture this is not properly understood by many. An individual's needs are not just food, clothing and shelter alone, but he also has to satisfy his emotional needs. One has to live in the society and depend on it for many things. Life will be smoother and happier if one interacts with his fellow beings in a proper manner. We should not develop hatred towards others. Hating people is like burning our own home to get rid of a rat.

Man is different from machines, computers and robots. He has emotions of love and care and he needs them. Only comforts and luxuries cannot give happiness. If we do not understand this, our relationships suffer. When persons are forced to live in isolation against their will without friends or companions, they tend to become unbalanced and mad.

Majority of the problems in a bad relationship arise due to lack of proper communication and understanding. Sometimes the problem may be that we do not express our feelings and thoughts to others. We feel it is none of their concern or that they do not understand what we feel. Talking or writing a letter is a simple and effective solution that can avert disasters in relationships. Hesitation to express may lead to loss of faith and trust. If the matter is important, it should be communicated in time, otherwise some differences may occur, hatred develops, communication stops and relationships suffer.

Care of Love

Every human being is unique. No two persons think or work alike. There is difference in the way people perceive things. The manner in which we deal with different persons is different and it varies. This makes every relationship unique and special.

The word "Love" was much liked after the word Mother. Love, perhaps the greatest force on earth, can make miracles. Love for peace can end wars and love for war can eliminate peace. Along with food, clothing and shelter, love is also a basic necessity. People need to feel that they are cared for. A genuine smile and a kind word can instil confidence when a person is in despair. When you tell a person that you care for him, it increases his self-worth, self-respect and confidence. We should make each day special with small acts of kindness and care.

Love is one word that every one knows, but it also may be the word least understood. Love does not mean lust or liking the opposite gender. It is a deep inner feeling of affection and liking. Love towards people requires inner growth. It requires maturity, understanding, broad-mindedness and experience. If you give love, you get love in return. We reap what we sow. We shall extend our love and friendship to get it in return. Sri Sathya Sai Baba preaches and insists on the care of love (*prema tattva*). He addresses the people as *prema svarupulara* meaning embodiments of love. Something can be achieved peacefully through love rather than through rights or fights.

Someone rightly said it does not matter if you have a million friends but we need a friend who stands by us when millions are against us. To get such a friend one needs to develop love, trust and understanding.

Relation with Juniors, Equals and Seniors

In most cases of community life, problems arise in one's relations with juniors, equals and sometimes with seniors. Clash of ego is one reason. Sometimes jealousy is the cause. We often face such negative aspects in day-to-day life. They are the hurdles in our progress. Sometimes, it is sheer immaturity and misunderstanding that plays havoc. We expect our juniors to immediately pick up what we say or instruct. We expect our seniors immediately to appreciate and act on our appeals or requests. Similar are our expectations in relationship with our servants, friends and others.

Egoism

The desire to argue and quarrel is a sign of ego. It is our ego that leads us to needless quarrels. More than happiness people want their point of view to be appreciated and accepted. Our success and experience lead us to ego. The egoism plays havoc in our personal relations. Lesser the ego, happier is the relationship with others. All love an ego-less child. When we grow up, our ego is centred on our works and achievements. We develop a feeling that we have done great things and better than others and therefore we deserve better name and reward. In this way our ego increases. As a result, we are struck by the feelings of anger, frustration and jealousy. And by these negative aspects, our relationships suffer.

Stubbornness is not strength. Stubbornness merely hides one's weakness. Strong is he who is flexible like steel and does not break. Strong is he who can live in harmony with many people and heed to opinions other than his own.

Increasing suicides, divorces, violence and petty quarrels indicate the pathetic condition of interpersonal relations driven by fragile egos. It is not arguments that win the hearts. It is not the displeasure that builds relations. It is only the love all the way that can do something to build good relations. The more we understand this the better will be our lives.

Projection of State of Being

Interpersonal relations are the manifestation of inner man. What a man does outside is the expression of his state of being. The more calm, deep, pure and integrated a person is in his inner life, the greater will be the expression of honesty, love, compassion and understanding in dealings with others. One is the cause and the other is the effect. Interpersonal relationships thus begin inside first. As a man thinks, so he becomes. If we think positively, we develop a positive outlook towards life, and vice versa. What is important for us to develop good human relationships is the fundamental change in our mindset. Our thoughts shape our life. Optimistic mind or positive mind changes not only our life, but it changes the environment around us.

Range of Interpersonal Relations

An important aspect in the life of a human being is the network of relations. We come across a great diversity of relationships in our lives. Some of the well-defined relationships, which play a major role in our life are mentioned hereunder:

- *Mother–Child relationship*: This is one of the most loving and dedicated relationships that we often see and experience. We find this not only among human beings, but also in the animal world.
- *Teacher–Student relationship*: This is significant, relevant and respectful.
- *Husband–Wife relationship*: In India, this is regarded as the most sacred and a great tie-up.
- *God–Devotee relationship*: It is the most exalted of all relationships.
- *Career relationships*: These are like
  - Client–Boss
  - Customer–Salesman
  - Citizen–State, etc.

These professional relationships depend purely on give and take. It is a kind of symbiosis through which both parties benefit.

Self-control

Gain control over oneself before gaining control over others. This is a time-tested principle. Only a person of controlled speech and conduct can have healthy relations. We generally expect something or other in return for everything we give. When this expectation is not met, it leads to frustration. Hence we have to balance these expectations. A lot of self-improvement and patience is essential to develop these traits.

We receive many good ideas from others, but we do not consider them and put them into practice. We do not put up hard work, which is the secret of success. Also sometimes we do not act on what we know. Hurry and speed spoils good relations. Overcoming our lower self, refining and purifying our mind, understanding the psychology of others, and allowing their preferences are essential in all situations and conditions.

Pleasantness in Talk

One should be careful while communicating with others to maintain pleasant relations. More often friendships were lost because of rashness in talk and use of harsh words. Unpleasant words cause injury, which no medicine can heal. Sometimes even time cannot heal it. It is said, even unpleasant truth should not be spoken in a harsh manner. It is great and graceful to use the right type of words in right situation at right time. Tongue does not have a bone but it can break the bones. Courtesy costs nothing, but earns goodwill. One should practise limited speech. It should be clear and to the point. Excessive talk may involve unnecessary issues and may lead to criticism, shouting and may end in quarrels and violence.

Parents' Role in Rearing Children

Parents' role is important in moulding children's personality. But most parents are not aware of how to nurture their children. They insist, seriously instruct and frighten the children in the name of discipline. They imbibe in their children the negative feelings, fear, failures keeping their children away from others. When the child is reluctant to take food, the mother shows some fierce items or some dark matters calling them as devils or spirits instilling fear in the child. Some parents scold and beat the children often instructing them to do something. Home is the first school to a child. Mother and father are the first teachers. A child learns and imitates its parents. Hence parents should know and learn how to rear and motivate their children.

To Live an Integrated Life

One main reason for not being able to maintain good relations is the inability of an individual to live an integrated life. One has to respond to different situations in one's life with the same qualities. The individual has to perform different roles in day-to-day life. These roles are like the best boss, best subordinate, best friend, best father/mother, best son/daughter and so on. An individual tries his most to play the best role in different situations. But, however, it is difficult and not possible to play the best role in all these situations with different selves.

We do not live our life with total integrity because of the fear of losing wealth, position, fame, etc. This is because the individual wants to play an ideal role set by himself, which he is unable to play or not allowed to do so.

The greatest of such managers is Lord Krishna, who managed every situation. He played the roles as the best friend to his friends, best husband to all his wives, best mediator (ambassador), best warrior and worst enemy to the enemies.

Conclusion

Our thoughts shape our life. Harmonious human relations can be a great source of happiness and lack of this produces intense agony leading to various physical and mental ailments.

A leading doctor said —

The real epidemic in our society is not only the physical heart disease, but it is the emotional and mental disease, that is, the deep feelings of loneliness, alienation, and depression that are prevalent now in our society, with the collapse of social structure of joint families that used to provide a sense of connection and bondage. It is the root cause of illness, cynicism, and violence in our society. Joint families and community living neutralize problems resulting from isolated living.

Interpersonal relations are much stressed and emphasized in India. It is said,

matrudevo bhava - Mother is god

pitrudevo bhava - Father is god

acharyadevo bhava - Teacher is god

atithidevo bhava - Guest is god

But now the man is becoming a slave to the machines and forgetting the values. Our present education system is not imparting human values and ethics. Now some people are already suffering from stress-related or psychiatric problems due to poor interpersonal relations. This can be reduced by managing good relations and by self-control. It is a fact that people live with others only to satisfy their personal and selfish mutual needs. Everyone is ultimately selfish. This includes all like husband–wife, parent–children, trader–customer or anyone.

Man needs man. Let us value the higher values like love, mutual respect and put into practice what good human relations we have learned from our ancestors.

7

Minding the Mind

THE first lesson in spirituality is not the thoughts on God, but it is managing the mind, so that it does not create problems by itself. One should develop control over his mind and senses. Otherwise disharmony develops in the life and one may lose belief in values. Hence minding the mind is the need of the day.

Mind plays many roles in one's life. If mind is there, the world and objects are there. Mind acts and reacts continuously and restlessly. The mind is fickle in nature and has the tendency of moving from one thought to another and hence it is necessary to observe the thought process. It should be kept well in condition, otherwise it may lead us to some miserable situations. The mind is not an inert matter. It is a storehouse of abundant energy into the depths of mind.

Our mind is our great treasure. We are the master and we are responsible to shape our mind as we like. We should avoid evil thoughts and bad associations and nourish the mind with higher ideals and noble thoughts. It is the thought that breeds suffering, anxiety and fear.

Mind is like a mad elephant. We may bathe it, but it rolls in the dust and makes itself unclean again. Therefore we must use many means to hold the mind. Our body, mind and senses are like untrained horses. Even if the desired comforts are given to the body, it is not satisfied. Mind always wants variety and new things. It goes on searching for new things or to create new things. We must learn to control the senses. Man has the power to guide them instead of being dragged by them this side or that side. Swamy Sukha Bodhananda says, "mind is the bundle of thoughts; more than heart attacks people suffer from thought attacks."

Our mind is our friend and also a foe. If we keep it under control, it is our great friend; otherwise it becomes our foe. Mind is the storehouse of thoughts and memories. It has the capacity for analytical, discriminative and rational thinking. The power of the mind causes attraction to the worldly attainments and its conquest makes the quest attainable. Mind's attention towards senses is to be kept under control of the intellect (*buddhi*).

Peace and pain are never associated. Peace and happiness go together. Peace is possible only when the mind is calm. Both happiness and sorrow are there in the mind. They are the reflections perceived by the mind. When the mind is tranquil and satisfied one feels happy. It is with the help of the mind that one can gain access to one's own self.

We look for the causes of our sufferings in the outer world, but we should look within ourselves and become aware of our thoughts. One's behaviour and attitude all depends on the psychology of the mind of the individual. Mind allocates work to the body parts and goes out on other thoughts. We often find that we do not apply our mind on the work that we do and we perform them mechanically. Hence the results may not be satisfying.

Though the senses respond to the activities to derive enjoyment, it is the mind that provokes the senses to act and ultimately it is the mind that enjoys or suffers. The senses are activated by the mind. Hence whatever is talked, it goes ultimately to the mind. The persons who enjoy more wealth, power and position get frustrations and disappointments in return. Mind is not satisfied with the available positions, it searches for something else. An agitated mind cannot understand the truth of the Reality. A calm and peaceful mind can understand and gets elevated to the higher levels of Consciousness.

The thoughts come first and action or reaction follows later. In all areas of work like science, technology, industry, fine arts and so on, the seeds of progress or change are born in the mind first. Our hopes, aspirations, feelings — good or bad — are the results of our thoughts. We should recognize how our mind influences our actions. In order to reach this understanding, we must cultivate pure and healthy mind.

We have to keep our body and mind both clean. Body cleanliness is external (*bahya suci*) and the mind cleanliness is internal (*antara suci*). Both these are interrelated. The cleanliness depends on the mind of the person. We see most of the people make the premises unclean. They litter the places and spit often here and there making the places unclean and unhealthy. Carelessness and indiscipline are their style of living. The cleanliness of a house and the premises speak the inner mind of the dwellers. This shows how orderly or disorderly is the user's approach to life.

An ideal person must be organized in all his actions and style of living. He should be clean and orderly. This is to be done not for external show or to please others. This should be for one's own sake and good.

Our behaviour reflects our state of mind. The way we speak, react, request or act, everything shows the state of our mind. Whether we live in a thatched hut or a palace, it does not matter. What matters is that we all live in our mind. Our mind is our first abode. It is the mind that shapes the body and our behaviour. Hence mind must be kept clean.

Our mind is restless most of the time. It is sad, angry, greedy and jealous. We feel that the outside situations disturb our mind. But why do we allow them to make our mind disturbed? We become upset because our mind is not under our control. Our mind is not trained and not put in the right position. As the competition is increasing outside, we should develop our capacity to deal with the situation. This requires moving and living with people in the society. For this, we should make proper adjustments and deal with the people properly, take their help, give our help and get mutual benefit. We should train and elevate our mind and cultivate the habit of extending our friendliness, compassion, and cheerfulness towards others.

If we love the work and the people, our mind gets adjusted to the situations and it slowly rises to the level of equanimity.

The decline of human societies could be disastrous as a consequence of pollution of individual's mind. Mind is unsteady and it is like polluted dirty water. In order to see through the water, it should be kept clean.

As is one's mind, so is he. What one feels and thinks, so he becomes. You reap what you sow. In Sanskrit it is said —

mano mulam jagat — Mind is the root cause of the world

mano kalpitam jagat — The world is as the mind dreams

Violence, crime and unhappiness are born due to lack of proper understanding. Often, we feel that we are good and right and others are bad and wrong. This feeling creates problems and unrest to the mind.

Material of this world provides only temporary pleasure and satisfaction. Even if all the pleasures are fulfilled, mind is not satisfied and it goes on searching for more. Then the question arises, "can the mind be satisfied or what can satisfy the mind?" Man was continuously in search of an answer to this question. This is an eternal question. The great scriptures, epics, and religions are revolving around this question. Then who can satisfy the mind? The answer for this is: It is none other than the mind alone. Mind alone can satisfy and control the mind. A thorn in foot can be removed only by another thorn.

The sacred text, *Yoga Vasishtha*, contains instructions using interesting contexts and valuable discussions.

The lord blessed the king Bali, the grandson of Prahlada. He reigned for many years with no worry. But he remained restless even in this satiated state. His mind sought something more lasting. He wondered whether there is any gain from all the riches. He craved for that which would lead him to eternal bliss, which is ultimate. Then Bali's father Virochana gave instructions to Bali on this. Virochana made it clear that the mind is the cause of these turbulences, bondage and miseries.

Mind-Control

This is a fundamental principle for developing and integrating our personality. This is applicable at every step in our life. It is controlling the mind and senses not going astray. This cannot be achieved in a short time in one stroke. It is a continuous process.

A good way to control the mind is to practise punctuality in time. We should plan our timetable priority-wise for our routine works and follow it strictly. Then our mind gets accustomed to it. Generally our mind rebels and tries to avoid or shirk with some reasons not to follow the timetable. But we must use our will power and practise to follow the time strictly.

Will Power — An Incident from the Life of Tulasidas

The will power or the strength of mind is so powerful that it leads the individual to any great extent. Here is an incident from the life of Sant Tulasidas to show the strength of mind.

Tulasidas in his youth was much attracted and attached to his wife and he neglected his duties. He was not able to separate himself from his wife. Once when he returned home he was depressed and felt unhappy to know that his wife had gone to her parents' house. His mother advised him to go in the morning, as it was raining heavily in that stormy night. Tulasidas did not heed his mother's advice and immediately rushed to his wife's house in that heavy rain.

A river separated the two villages and it was in floods at that time. There was not a single person visible in that dark stormy night. In the river he found something floating on the water and he took hold of it and crossed the river to the other bank. Though he knocked at the door of her house, no one could hear him in that heavy rain and loud thunders. In order to gain entry into the compound he took hold of what appeared as a rope, climbed it and got inside. His wife could not believe her eyes when her husband stood in front of her in the dead of that night. The good lady took him in and offered hospitality.

It was later known that what he thought of a rope was a python and the floating thing in the river water, which he used to cross the river, was a corpse.

It is the serious desire in the mind of Tulasidas that led him to his wife in that deadly night. Hence one with strong will-power can reach to any extent. Later the wife of Tulasidas casually remarked that he would realize God if he had the same ardent desire for the Immortal God. This has brought an instant transformation in Tulasidas. Thanks to his wife's sincere advice by which Tulasidas became a renowned saint who composed the immortal devotional classic, *Ramacharitmanas*.

There is a question, "Who can conquer the world?" The answer is: he who conquers his mind.

If mind is restless and sorrowful, then even a healthy body loses its strength, and its health is spoiled. But if the mind is charged with inspiration, enthusiasm and hope, then even a frail and lean bodied one can do wonders.

Mind Strength and Faith — A Story

One day when sage Narada was on his usual rounds, a saint (*sanyasi*) who has been doing meditation for a long time called Narada and asked — "O Narada! You know I left my family and am doing penance since long time to attain liberation (*moksha*) from lives. I think I am nearing my goal to get liberation. O Narada! please ask Brahma and tell me when I will get salvation from my lives." Then after some days Narada appeared before the *sanyasi* and said, "you get liberation in a few hundreds of births and deaths."

The *sanyasi* felt much unhappy, annoyed and chided himself and the God and told Narada, "I am doing penance for long years, I am a sincere devotee of the God, the God is not kind enough on me at all, God has become stubborn, tough and stone, he is not listening to me at all."

This was the state of mind of the *sanyasi*. After this incident, the *sanyasi* felt that anyway he has to live for some hundreds of lives, hence doing penance now in this life is unnecessary and left penance and lived unhappily. Here *sanyasi* could not understand the essence of the reality at all. He thought that he gets something after his death, which he is calling liberation (*mukti*). He could not understand that liberation is not a stage or life or something available after death. One has to attain the freedom and liberation in the mind when he is alive in the world, which is called *jeevan mukti*.

In another case, a cobbler is doing his duty of making leather items. When Narada appeared before him, the cobbler asked Narada, "O Narada! You are a great sage and you know everything, you know the lives of all. Please tell me, when do I get liberation?" Narada said, "you have to live still some thousands of births to get salvation."

Then the cobbler immediately fell at the feet of Narada and paid his respects. The cobbler felt much happy, delighted and started dancing and singing. "O God! you are so kind to me. I have to live only a few thousands of lives to reach you and to join you. The time to reach you is short. O My God! thank you very much, you are very kind, you can do anything, I am not able to digest this overbound happiness." The cobbler sang, danced with boundless happiness praising the Lord and left his life on the spot enjoying infinite bliss and got liberated immediately.

Here the cobbler is attending his normal responsibilities (*karma*) with full trust and faith on God in his mind. He is happy and positive attitude-oriented. Hence by this state of mind, the cobbler achieved liberation. Whereas, in the previous case, the *sanyasi* developed an egoistic tendency that he is doing some favour to God in doing penance. Hence he failed finally with misfaith. One has to understand well the moral in this story.

Characteristics of Mind (Gunas)

There are three characteristics in the mind broadly. These three exist in every human being. Different quantities (doses) of these *gunas* determine different mindsets. These *gunas* are tamas, rajas and sattva.

TAMAS MIND

The *tamas* mind is lazy, dull, sluggish and averse to mental work. Such persons lack initiative in their action. They avoid hard work especially mental work. They spend a leisurely life and waste time. They do not hesitate to hurt others and do not help. They get sadistic pleasure by causing violence and disturbing peace. This is the lower level of mind and is an animal nature.

RAJAS MIND

The mind here is active and selfish. Such persons are egoistic and they work hard for personal gains, sensual pleasure and wealth. They help others for some benefits in return. They demand their rights. These people are middle category and they are of human nature.

A good deal of *rajas* works bring benefit to the people. These works include setting up of educational institutions, industries, hospitals, roads, infrastructure, places of worship, gardens, etc. all involving much effort. But all these are done with profit motive. These activities are affected by fear of failure of projects, conflicts with people causing worry, anxiety, anger, frustration and ill-health. There is no ultimate happiness. But these actions are better than *tamas* actions.

SATTVA MIND

The mind is active but under control. Such persons are always right, straightforward, rational, fearless, serene and calm. They help others. The *sattva* mind doer performs works without attachment, likes or dislikes and without any desire. He is free from ego. He enjoys inner happiness and excellence in work and promotes mental and physical health. This is divine nature.

Control of Mind

A well-controlled and disciplined mind is necessary even to acquire ordinary knowledge in different fields of learning. It is difficult to control the mind, but it is not impossible. It can be brought under control by constant practice (*abhyasa*) and dispassion (*vairagya*). Here dispassion means leaving all the work and possessions or looking everything as a waste — this is not correct. Hard work, dexterity, persistence, controlling passions and punctuality in time bring control of mind. We should carefully handle the mind and remain free from depression, tension and excitements.

Regular Practice (Sadhana)

More knowledge or mere knowledge of making a product does not give the product. It has to undergo the total making process with the required material and time to get the final product. Sri Ramakrishna Paramahansa said, knowledge that milk contains butter does not give you the butter. It involves the process like boiling the milk, then seeding it with curd and after its cooling, keeping it undisturbed for the required time and then churning the curd. Then you get the butter floating on the buttermilk. The mind that has been trained by regular practice will develop steadfastness and will not swing by other disturbances.

It is not enough to condemn the darkness. There should be the act of bringing light to dispel the darkness. Your own initiative and action are necessary to fulfil the required task.

Controlling the mind in our daily life is possible by practising the following disciplines regularly:

- Slowly reduce and overcome the desires especially the sensual pleasures, name, fame, etc.
- Associate in the company of good saints, attend

spiritual meetings or other useful ideal activities, maintain good relations with people.

- Practise discrimination, judgement, dispassion and detachment in a cool, calm manner.
- Engage yourself in fair and ideal occupations with fair dealings with people.
- Practise simple respiratory exercises (*pranayama*) and meditation daily by following the discipline exercises of *ashtangayoga* (eightfold paths): *yama, niyama, asana, pranayama, pratyahara, dharana, dhyana* and *samadhi*.

Mind needs lot of nurture, education and motivation to make it elevated to higher planes of thinking. Hence we must mind our mind.

8

The Spirit of Universe

THERE is a great potential power (*shakti*) in this universe, which is all-pervading and not seen. Without this power even a small leaf does not move. People call this power by different names like God, the Lord, Ishvara, *Atma*, *Brahman*, Truth, Reality, Changeless, Almighty, Formless, Ever-changing, Pure Consciousness, Birthless, Deathless and so on. The reality is Akshara (destructionless). There is nothing in this universe devoid of this.

The universal power cannot be seen in its basic form with ordinary eyes and the world cannot exist without it. Hence we should not come to a determination or conclusion that because the great power is not seen or cannot be seem, it does not exist. Science insists on empirical, testable and demonstrable protocols. There are many, which are not seen, but exist. Radio waves, x-rays and electric power exist, but cannot be seen. There are large numbers of electrical appliances. All of them are working and the power behind them is electricity, but it is not seen. The stars are visible only in the night. Hence can we say that stars do not exist in day time?

The great potential life-giving soul (*prana*) is not seen, but we firmly know that it exists and is functioning in the live bodies and exits from the body at the time of death. This power is too subtle and it cannot be touched, tasted, seen, heard or smelled. We know that we do the act of eating, but we do not know who or what digests the food in the stomach. We do not know how we grow. We cannot even explain what are thoughts and how do they arise. Most of these have no evidence. They have to be wisely imagined, understood and have to be trusted with faith.

The material world is the manifestation or revelation of the Almighty *Atma*. The whole universe is the body of that infinite power. This power cannot be said as either male or female. It is genderless. Worldly objects and species are recognized by form, quality, function and relationship, but the Supreme Reality cannot be defined by such criteria.

The light illumines the objects, but is different from them. Similarly the *atma* reveals the bodies, but is distinct from them. These revelations are continuous, ever-changing and moving. Nothing is constant in this universe, but ever-changing is constant. But the changing objects are not permanent. The potential behind these changing objects is changeless and permanent. To be free from sorrows we should shift our focus from change to changeless. The knowledge of the self (*atma*) makes one beyond sorrows.

Some call this great potential as God. But here the word God is misleading often. People imagine and understand God like a superhuman carrying some mystical weapons and living in the high skies. Believing God in such form may mislead the seeker. The reality can be imagined in any form or without a form. If a devotee intensely believes in the form, the mighty power may manifest in that form.

When Hiranyakasipu asks his son Prahlad where lord Narayana resides, Prahlad replies that lord resides everywhere. Lord is all-pervading (Sarvantaryami). Lord resides in an atom and even if an atom is split into parts, lord still resides in every part of those smallest parts of atom.

Whatever the miracles or blessings one enjoys, it is only due to the cause of innate and intense devotion or one-pointed thinking of the devotee. The appearance of God to an ardent devotee is not by external source, but it is certainly by a force driven from inside by the deep and intense thinking and innate urge of the devotee. One has to go beyond the mind into the realm of faith to understand these subtle truths. Though the supreme reality is all-pervading, it is too subtle to recognize in gross aspects. This truth remains beyond the grasp of the senses. Mind can recognize the external objects only. The subtle truths can be recognized only by strong inner conviction.

People's understanding level is different. Hence literature and scriptures were made in various ways for their use. Capacity of understanding varies from one to other and this leads to multiple interpretations and beliefs.

The universe can be imagined in two divisions. One is the visible world (matter), which is ever-changing and destructible. The other is the subtle potential sustaining this universe, which is changeless and formless. If a man separates himself from the matter, he becomes formless without the finite lines. Formless means it is infinite and all-pervading with no dimension, size and shape. This is the Reality and Spirit of this universe. It is one undivided, formless, size-less, omnipresent super power.

The physical eyes or the senses cannot perceive the truth of the universal power. It is to be gained through wisdom, perception, discrimination and experience. The realized souls can see beyond the world and beyond the universe. They recognize that the doer in the body is the self, which is identical with supreme Self (the Reality).

A person being driven by ego with impure mind who is immersed in material world cannot perceive this truth. The failure on the part of an individual to recognize a tree or a flower does not indicate a fault in the object. It lies in the deficiency of the person. Truth remains as truth forever, even if it is not recognized or understood. It is for the individual to understand this.

The senses, mind and intellect are meant to understand the world and the potential lying behind this creation. But it is not easy to realize the truth by ordinary vision. The wealth, possessions, attainments, etc. make the individual move away from the truth leading towards ignorance of truth.

Every individual should recognize that whatever material and intellectual attainments everyone of us possesses have come to us from the universal power and hence we should remain ever grateful to that force without any sense of ego. This can be achieved only by the practice of training the mind through constant study, learning and through meditation. One has to transcend the human faculties to understand the truth (*atma*). One's attainments are important than one's birth or status.

In some of the houses, an interesting poster is displayed, which says:

> *God is the head of this house.*
> *He is the unseen guest at every meal and is a silent listener in every conversation.*

Hence we have to stop criticizing others, should not indulge in cheap gossip and not waste our time in meaningless pursuits.

9

Vishvarupa (The Universe)

THE universe in which we are living and which we are seeing is the family of our Sun. It is definitely amazing and surprising to know that the universe contains most miraculous objects, working and sustaining depending on each other. It is a unique system working in unity as a team. The entire universe is in flux. It is in continuous motion, charge, flowing and discharging. Let us look into the objects of this universe.

Our solar system (family) contains the following planets in sequence from the Sun.

Planet	Rotation time	Length of year	Number of satellites
Mercury	59 days	88 days	0
Venus	249 days	224.7 days	0
Earth	23.9 days	365.3 days	1
Mars	24.6 hours	687 days	2
Jupiter	9.8 hours	11.9 years	13
Saturn	10.2 hours	29.5 years	9
Uranus	10.8 hours	84 years	5
Neptune	15 hours	164.8 years	2
Pluto	6.4 days	248.8 years	0

Courtesy: Earth Science by F. Martin Brown & Wayne Bailey

These planets are self-rotating and are revolving around the Sun in separate elliptical orbits continuously. Each planet has its different body material, size, volume, colour and distance from the Sun. Each planet has its different orbit and speed in rotation and movement. These planets have their own moons revolving around them and moving along with them.

The Sun is the largest and is a gaseous burning body. Sun is self-luminous, i.e. it shines by its own power. It is a gigantic ball of hot gases. Its radius is 109 times that of the earth. Its volume is over a million times greater than the earth's. But its density is less than a third of the earth, as it is a gaseous object. Its diameter is 12,88,000 km. It has no solid surface. Sun is essential to the life on earth. It provides all the energy to the earth.

The solar family contains mainly the nine planets, their satellites, comets, meteors and asteroids, minor planets and beyond these are stars and black holes.

Largest planet in this Solar system is Jupiter. Its diameter is around eleven times that of the earth. Mercury is the smallest.

Earth is a great natural abode with atmosphere and with living bodies. There are countless different varieties of species living on earth. Hence Lord Krishna said in *Bhagavad-Gita*, "I am the reality and I am manifest with innumerable heads, mouths, arms, limbs, etc." Thousands of species were extinct earlier and the present available species may be exterminated after some time and new species will arrive in due course.

It is said, there are countless Suns and Universes beyond this universe. We are not able to know and understand our Sun and our universe. Then how can we understand other Suns and universes? Why up to there? We do not still know most miracles of our own planet earth. Last but not least, we are not able to know the miracles of our own body system. Hence it is our minimum duty and *dharma* that we should know the greatness of our own body and the mind. If this is known, everything is known.

The living entities (*jiva*s) on the earth are minute samples of the supreme Reality. Human body is made from the planets of Universe and it is a Universe in miniature. All that exists in the Universe also exists in human body and further the essence of whole Universe exists in an atom.

Fullness of Universe

The world is full (*purnam*) to its fullest extent. There is no dearth of anything anywhere. There is no creation or destruction of any material in this universe. One mass is changed to the other. The products made by man are just some mixes and additions of some materials available on earth. By mixing of different materials various products are made. In this process, the heating and cooling energies are used. If a material is burnt, we feel that it is destroyed. But in fact it is not destroyed, it is converted into other energies like heat energy, carbon dioxide, other gaseous substances and ash, etc.

In this nature nothing can be created or nothing can be destroyed. One form of energy or mass is changed to another. This is the law of nature and conservation of mass and energy. Mass can be converted into energy and conversely energy can be converted into mass. German scientist Einstein asserted that energy itself has mass. If mass is destroyed, a great deal of energy would be released. This resulted in the creation of atom bomb.

The divine is full (*purnam*). Even if something is added to the full, it is full. If something is removed from this full, it is still full. This fullness is described here in a verse in Sanskrit language as:

purnamadah purnamidam purnat purna mudacyate ।
purnasya purnamaadaaya purna mevavasishyate ॥

There is no deficiency of anything in this nature. If at all any deficiency is found, it is man-made and created. It is up to the man to choose, select, elect and act.

The universe described here is the manifestation of the supreme Reality. It is the Vishvarupa, the reflection of God. Lord Krishna explained and showed this form to Arjuna; this cannot be seen wholly in detail by ordinary eyes. The sustaining superpower of this great Vishvarupa is the supreme Reality, the *atma* or the God.

10

Satsang (Good Company)

In this world no creature or species can live alone without having its companions. Man is not separate form this. Rich or poor have to live with the people, amidst people, by (help from) the people, for the people and alongside the people. All the people are not alike. There are different people with different thoughts and experiences, good or bad. Our behaviour largely depends on the environment of our family, friends, where we live or where we were nurtured from childhood. The environment influences much and sets the mindset of the individual. Hence one's association with the people plays an important role in moulding the character of a person. Everyone must live in the company of holy men. It is necessary for all including *sanyasis* (ascetics). The word *satsang* means good environment or good company.

Association with holy teachers and holy people helps well in one's effort to remove ignorance, while association with evil-minded people is harmful and destructive. One with a sinful heart will never find peace. The only way to peace is to engage oneself in good deeds, good thoughts and good words. Think good, speak good, act good and be good. Always remember ABC (Avoid Bad Company) and practise the culture of respecting others. One has to get over the ill feelings towards others. One should be honest and assess one's inner thoughts in this regard.

We must read and study the lives of great people. We shall live in their company and breathe the atmosphere of purity and goodness, which is sure to fill us with energy, vigour and aspiration. Environment leaves hard impressions on the persons who live in those surroundings. If you live with dogs you will learn how to howl and bark. Our mind moulds according to the company that we keep.

People who live in filthy environment forget cleanliness and they are accustomed to the filth. The prisoners who are habituated to jail environment do not want to leave the jail. Such is the influence of habits and environment. Hence we must be cautious of environment in which we live.

Living in the company of good saints leads to progress towards peace. The company of mature-minded saints brings changes in the mind and lifts it from its baser tendencies.

A hungry man's immediate need is only food, so also a thirsty man satisfies himself by drinking water. Likewise if a seeker who wants peace of mind engages in the company of holy people, he gets changed and purified.

Association with holy people and listening to holy lessons will show you a way. People are valuable than the wealth of the world. So we have to live, associate, help, get help and make great men. The teacher cannot take you till the destination. You have to undertake the grand journey by yourself. One's association with people, good or bad, will certainly influence one's course of life. The company of good is likely to augment one's mental and living progress. The bad influence leads to downfall.

Just like our bodies need good food everyday, our minds also need good thoughts and listening everyday. We need to feed our mind with pure and positive thoughts to stay on the right track.

A householder has the right to spend his spare time anywhere, but it is ideal for him to join and work in a spiritual, cultural, or any worthy organization, so that he can lead a useful and contented life with a meaning.

Vivekananda advocated service that can be extended in four ways: by providing food (*anna*), health (*prana*), education (*vidya*) and spiritual knowledge (*jnana*). Such service is worship of God in man. By developing this outlook all work can be transformed into worship of God.

Our participation with people on various occasions gives us information and knowledge which we cherish. We honour invitations to weddings, birthdays and like occasions. But some people keep away on occasions of death. In fact, death also is an occasion. In *Ramayana*, Lord Rama performed last rites to the bird Jatayu. Was Rama related to Jatayu? Did he not feel the responsibility of doing the rites to the bird? Vibhishana refused to perform the last rites to his brother Ravana for Ravana's wickedness. But Rama persuaded Vibhishana to do this duty without considering the bad deeds of Ravana.

One cannot live alone without the help of others. Hence one has to cultivate the good habit of participating in good associations. The benefits here are learning knowledge from others, a way to serve others and to share with others.

A good attribute one has to practise is humbleness. Trees laden with fruits are humble. The people with knowledge are humble. Just as the unyielding dry stick snaps, an arrogant person who does not bend and who is not humble is finally destroyed. All is well that ends well. Swami Tatvavidananda Saraswati in a lecture once said, it is better to say that all is well that bends well.

There are good organizations that are imparting moral education, love, peace and Vedanta philosophy. Sri Sathya

Sai Baba has been spreading peace and love across the world with spiritual and social service activities irrespective of religion. He taught the world the real value of love, peace and service. He preached that everyone has to be good irrespective of one's religion.

The most ideal organizations like Sri Ramakrishna Mission, Sri Sathya Sai Baba organizations, Ramana Maharshi Ashram, Swami Dayananda Ashram, Swami Chinmayananda Mission, Isha Foundation and many more other organizations are imparting good education, moral values and Vedanta philosophy. One must participate in such worthy organizations, learn well and become an elite person and enjoy the value of life.

Reading

Reading is to the mind what exercise is to the body. Books are great companions. One can spend any amount of one's lifetime in reading books. Great knowledge can be acquired and it can be imparted to others. Books are the records of men's great thoughts and valuable experiences. They disseminate valuable information continuously for generations together. One who does not read books has no advantage over the one who cannot read or write. Everyday one must read some ideal and useful matter especially like *Bhagavad-Gita* or the gospels of great men.

11

State of Equanimity

LIFE is a mix of joy and sorrow. One should learn to treat both these with equanimity. Success or failure depends on this equanimity. Lord Krishna explained this at great length and conferred highest acclaim to strong willed (*dhira*) or man of wisdom (*sthitaprajna*) who is able to maintain equanimity at all times. This is the highest state of mind and a trait that helps to cultivate discrimination. Equanimity of mind (*sama chittatvam*) is keeping the mind calm with no regard to external situations. Equanimity of mind is *yoga*. This is the status of a *jnani*. We cannot make a person a *jnani*. It has to come from within a person.

The state of equanimity in mind is attained only by determined and untiring effort. Lord Rama's exemplary behaviour both when the kingdom was offered and later when taken away represents this state of mind. This serves as a best example of inspiration and highest patience to all who wish to understand and cultivate this trait. Lord Rama was educated in Yoga from the Guru and sage Vasishtha. This Yoga and Rama's education was narrated well in the book *Yoga Vasishtha*.

Lord Krishna, Buddha, Jesus and Mohammad symbolized what humans can become. They showed us a great path as to what we can be. We should follow the path shown by them truly.

The dominant three characteristics (*gunas*) play the role in us. The first is animal nature (*tamas*) which is yielding to instinct. The next is human nature (*rajas*) which shows refined sensibilities and distinguishment. And the highest is the divine nature (*sattva*), which endows a person to see everyone as the Supreme Reality (*atma*). All these three qualities abide in every individual. By the use of intellect (*buddhi*) and proper discrimination (*viveka*), one can transform the criminal nature in man to the human nature and then to divine level.

Pure Consciousness

A form or a figure is something made by some material bounded by lines occupying some space and as such it is finite. If the perceiver separates him from the matter, he becomes formless and is infinite. When it is infinite, it is all in all and everything. Then one can see the truth everywhere either in form or in formlessness. Limitations are boundaries created in our minds. If a perceiver imagines himself formless and matter-less, he is left with pure consciousness away from the material world. This is the highest knowledge and the true understanding of the truth. Here matured imagination and self-experience are more important than knowledge. In meditation, this formless consciousness is to be experienced.

This subject needs a higher level of mental state and understanding. It cannot be taught. One has to pass through all different stages in evolution in one's life. It is a gradual progression. One of the main principles to keep equanimity is eradication of barriers. Human body is the *kshetra* (land) and one can use it consciously by the power of discrimination and get the richest and ripest reap.

One has to keep him balanced in all aspects of life. He should be moderate in his behaviour and live an active life. One should keep aloof from emotions, keep the thoughts balanced and should achieve a state of mind free from likes, dislikes and prejudices leading to *jnana*. The real spiritualists are those who are conscious of the potential power of *atma* which is the true Reality of Cosmos.

He who strives to rise above likes and dislikes develops a mindset not to hurt or cause pain to others. His behaviour changes altogether. The world's happenings and affairs do not distract him.

One should overcome and neutralize the feelings of pleasure and pain. Such neutralization is possible only by determined effort. One should practise and elevate his thoughts by hypnotizing himself as shown below and keep his mind fresh and joyous:

- I know that I am not this body, my real "I" is Reality, which is eternal
- This Reality is shining in me. It is *atma chaitanya*
- I see all the problems of this life (*samsara*) equally
- There is no ignorance in me
- All that need to be gained is gained and there are no gains or losses

The person who is above these mundane worldly affairs is a *jivanmukta* (free while living), *sthitahprajna* (of steady intellect), *trigunatita* (one who transcends three *guna*s of nature). After intense spiritual practice an aspirant can reach this state.

To get enlightenment one has to let off the negative vices, emotions, desires, etc. from oneself by acquired knowledge and *jnana*. Sri Jiddu Krishnamurthy, a great philosopher, has said — There is no path or methodology or theory that leads to self realization. Anything is binding. Rise above that and seek the truth.

This equanimity of mind is possible only by knowledge, awareness and high mental experience.

12

Detachment (Renunciation)

THE tendency to renounce attachment with the world leads a person towards high spiritual levels. *Bhagavad-Gita* shows how to get involved in the world and also remain detached. Sri Ramakrishna Paramahamsa quotes the analogy of the boat. The boat shall be in water, but the water must not be in the boat. It means that we should live in this world but not allow the world to get into us. Swami Sukha Bodhananda says, we may have all the comforts of life and still be comfortably miserable. It means that though we have all the comforts, we are not mentally comfortable or satisfied.

In times of facing vicissitudes of life a person develops detachment or dispossession. But this does not last long. As a fox blames the grapes that it could not reach as sour, likewise a person's detachment born out of frustration is short-lived. The mind can experience lasting peace only when there is total detachment. Detachment is not indifference and apathy towards others or our duties. It is detachment from one's passions, whims and fancies and all forms of selfishness.

Man came naked into this world from mother's womb and he leaves this world naked after death. Our journey is from womb to tomb. Even after our death, society goes in its own way. We cannot take any piece of bone of our body with us anywhere. A person working in a mint or a bank handles lakhs of rupees, but he cannot take a rupee when he goes out.

When we study geography, we read about so many rivers, mountains, and forests that we feel we cannot count them or cannot imagine the size. But when we study a book on universe or astronomy, the physical features of the earth and its size seem to be too little. Hence we should think big and become big enough to drown small differences and difficulties. Then inner calm is attained.

Hence when we think of our life, all the concerns are binding on us. When we think beyond this on eternity and on omniscience the bindings of the life becomes meagre. When we grow and when new subjects or objects are recognized, the early fascinations slowly fade away. The goal in our life will be changing. The goal changes depending on one's age, education, mental status, needs, social and cultural factors. If one understands the value of salvation, the world's happenings no longer seem to attract.

The living bodies are made up of food. Without food they cannot survive. The human body is totally a pervious jelly with innumerable sweat holes in the skin and there are nine organ openings from which the filth from the body emanates. We are too much fascinated and attached to this physical body and nurturing it with full fervour and fashion. Here it does not mean that the body should be neglected. The human body is a wonderful instrument. We must keep it clean, healthy and simple. Our body is a temple in which a divine spark is shining.

We have to prioritize our needs. We should be ready and practise to live a simple living. How to do this? If we are hungry, food is the immediate priority. Here food means it is not a food containing sweets and savouries. These are not a must. Food is necessary for life, but not a spicy food.

Even without these spices one can enjoy simple food, which fulfils hunger and help in the sustenance of life.

Likewise, showy ornamental utensils, vessels of silver and gold, and expensive furniture do not serve the purpose. Costly cots and beds are not necessary for sleeping on. A tired person gets sleep and sleeps anywhere. The external decorations are only to please our ego. The showcase items like idols, images, display articles, showpieces do not serve any purpose or give any comfort or utility. They are meant for exhibitionism and ego-satisfaction.

This means that the useful and utility items are a must and one should not be worried much in getting useless showy items. A house is a necessity to live in and it is also essential that it should be kept clean and airy.

By simple living our life will be in contentment. We can become a role model to the people. Desires and needs are different. Do not confuse your desires for needs. Needs are just basic essentials only. Hence do not be crazy to run after possessions. Birds and animals have no house or bank balance, yet they are happy. Man inspite of all the comforts is not happy.

If we do not have what we desire, let us make the best use of what we have with us. A great artist creates a masterpiece with ordinary material. It is not the material that makes an artist, but it is the artist who shapes the material. Artists use simple materials that are available in general.

Here in detachment, it is not the object that is important, it is the feeling and intention behind it is important. The feeling of detachment towards objects and possessions is important.

Detachment is a state of aloofness or indifference to people, surroundings, happenings, opinions, etc. Renunciation is an act of surrender or give-up. Contentment is satisfaction with what one possesses. It is a satisfied state. Some feel that contentment makes man dull, inactive and lazy, creating an obstacle to life's progress. Some say that contentment is the escape route to inefficient persons. Detachment and contentment are to the mind. One must not escape from his duties and responsibilities in the name of detachment and contentment. One can use and utilize all his possessions in life, but with detached mind. Detachment relaxes the mind.

Examples of discontentment are many. Ravana was a great warrior, but he could not control his inner being and as a result he failed and faced shameful death. Other examples are Duryodhana, Kamsa, and Shishupala; all are intelligent and competent, but failed due to their greediness and discontentment.

Sometimes chasing after the impossible, we may lose what is in our hand. In this modern era, Hitler, a great warrior, had no real need to establish his reign or control over whole of Europe. He led a victory over many nations. But still not satisfied, he waged war against Russia, which became costly, and he suffered defeat and a great loss. The greed and discontentment of Hitler made lakhs of people perish, and economy plunged. He lost everything that was there in his hands.

One is eligible to enjoy whatever is given by God. One gets his eligible share of possessions and should not consider them as personal possessions. If one really enjoys the possessions, but not attached to them, he slowly gets transformed and keeps himself detached. This is to be practised slowly.

One of Newton's laws states that for every action there is equal and opposite reaction. This is very true in every situation. Every effort gives some result. To get some benefit one must bear some loss. Swami Tattvavidananda Saraswati explained this well in his *Bhagavad-Gita* sermons. One gets articles (goods) only after losing valuable money. A bachelor gets the benefit of married life but he loses the freedom of bachelor life. To get the benefit of a *sanyasi* life one should lose the benefits of married life. A trader gets profit at the cost of goods. A student gets benefit of passing examination after losing lot of time and sleep. To win a game one should sweat. Finally a person who does not do anything gets the benefit of leisure, but loses his health and abilities. Everywhere the situation lies like this only. Hence there is no situation which fetches only the benefit (result) without losing something (effort). This is the law of nature. This is Karma Yoga. In this universe mass and energy are reciprocal. Nothing can be created or destroyed. One energy changes to another.

One cannot escape from life actions. Hence one should perform the ordained duties perfectly but in a detached way with a spirit of dedication to the Reality. One should be satisfied with whatever gains one gets. This mental practice of detachment greatly influences the individual, and his mind acts with equanimity towards the problems of the world.

Our success and achievements in the worldly affairs make us more egoistic. We feel proud of our possessions. But we do not know what happens in the next moment. We are unable to take with us any of our possessions like our breath, a rupee or a coin, or our dear ones or a part of our own physical body. We have to leave everything all of a sudden against our will.

Detachment is psychological and is a mental state. Mere spiritual knowledge may not help detachment. The purpose of this knowledge is to attain a state of detachment with regard to worldly matters. Detachment springs from one's sense of discrimination — the ability to recognize what is permanent and ever-lasting.

Though one lives in the family (*samsara*), he can move away from the world mentally and can become an observer of life. Detachment can well be compared to the best example of lotus. Lotus has its roots in the mud and it gets its nutrients from the mud and it grows. But it does not show any trace of mud — its petals and flowers are clean and neat.

13

Divine is Within

EVERY part of the universe is pulsating with great internal energy, which is the cause of existence and sustenance of this material world. Different people understood this great invisible potential in different ways. In every individual there is an identity called "I". Who is this real "I"? Is it one's body, mind or intellect recognized in relation to one's name or status? Or is it the inner self (*atma*) that is free, immortal and unattached? Yes. It is the self — the Reality (*atma*) or divine spirit that is the common denominator pervading all over the creation. As butter exists in milk, oil in sesame seeds and fire in wood, so the self exists in everyone. But individuals in association with the physical body are not able to identify the real nature. It is the self, which is the light within, which illumines and serves in all one's activities. Our body is an abode of divine spirit. It must be kept clean and disciplined.

People search for happiness in the outside world. But it is seldom found. The happiness is surely within us. Inner content is important than the container. The valuable jewels are important than the jewel box. The inner letter is valued than the envelope. The musk deer searches all around for its fragrance without realizing that the fragrance is emanating from its own body. Like that, out of ignorance man is searching in the outside world for joy, unaware of the fact that the source of bliss is within him. Also it is like a person searching for his spectacles outside, which are there on his nose. It is important to develop an insight to see everything as the manifestation of the Reality (self) and to perceive the self in all. This is not knowledge to acquire, one should experience it. We should be conscious of our inherent divinity and perfection.

Self-realization is the state of an elevated mind. This is *jnan*. By this one can discriminate the real and the unreal. This does not have anything to do with external objects. This is an inner transformation. The desire to know and see the Reality is latent in all of us, but it is submerged in our worldly pursuits. The sciences like Vedas, astronomy, philosophy are all secondary and the highest knowledge is knowing the truth of Universe or the self.

Inner Environment

The inner environment is the root cause of all activities. Are we able to control the inner environment? Lust, anger, greed, pride and envy are misleading us towards arrogance and selfishness. However technologically advanced we may be, or however fabulously rich we may be having all the amenities of life, if we are not mentally sound, it is a great irony to our life.

We know the world of sensations, but have no mastery over the inner world of thoughts and feelings, because we do not pay attention to it.

The human body is a combination of different sheaths (*kosha*s) like external body (*annamaya*), vital energy (*pranamaya*), mind (*manomaya*), intellect (*vijnanamaya*) and bliss (*anandamaya*). The Divine is something beyond all these.

Generally we have a concept of God as something finite, something we can measure. Absolute Reality abides in every living being all the time when it is alive. There is no need to search for it as if it is hidden somewhere. The true realization is to see this Reality everywhere and in everything. One has to realize the truth that the ultimate Reality is within everyone. This Reality which we worship is manifest in all the aspects of creation.

The divine Reality exists in me, in you and everywhere. We have to perceive the God in all the beings. Hence it is said:

- I am the divine/Reality - *aham brahma asmi*
- You are that - *tat tvam asi*
- Everywhere this reality is - *sarvam khalu idam brahma*

Every individual is supreme Reality. Man is divine enveloped in body. Prahlad saw the divinity as an inner being in all the creation including his father Hiranyakashipu. Human body is a vital instrument live and active. Everything lies in this body including the Reality. But man out of ignorance is wandering outside in search of God and peace. We are not aware of our true nature and self. Every human being is a unique fusion of spirit and matter.

It is said that the Reality is omnipresent, all-pervading and everlasting. It is unwise to search for this in worshipping places or in outside world. This requires a search inward, within a person. The visually handicapped lady Helen Keller said, the best and most beautiful things in this world cannot be seen or even touched. They must be felt with heart.

Lord Krishna stressed on this to Arjuna in *Bhagavad-Gita* as follows.

yachchhapi sarva bhutanam bijam tad aham arjuna,
na tad asti vina yat syath maya bhutam characharam.

O Arjun! I am the seed of all living beings. There are no beings either moving or non-moving without having me.

— *Bhagavad-Gita,* 10.39

As the Reality is prevailing in us, hence the body is said to be a temple. *Atma* dwells in all the beings in the form of inner being (*antaryamin*). Hence the body should not be abused or neglected, in which a deity the *atma* is consecrated. Nothing can be done and experienced without this body. The body cannot survive without this *atma*.

Hence with this idea, the temples are built with a body and a deity the *antaryamin*.

In the *Mantra Pushpam*, the existence of this *antaryamin* is explained as

> *nilato yada madhyastha dvidyullekheva bhasvara* ।
> *nivara suka vatthanvi pitha bhasvathyanupama* ॥

> In the midst of digestive fire (*jatharagni*) in the bodies, there is a small flame, which is burning vertically. It is illuminating like a lightning in dark clouds. Within this, a small flame is there:

> *tasya shikhaya madhye paramatma vyavastitaha* ।
> *sa brahma sa siva sa hari sa indra sa aksharaha parama svarat* ॥

> The divine exists in the middle of the head of this flame. It is Brahma, it is Shiva, it is Vishnu, it is Indra and it is non-destroyable (*akshara*) Supreme Being.

> *Svetasvatara Upanishad* quotes the following verse.

> *eko devaha sarva bhuteshu goodah*
> *sarva vyapi sarva bhutantaratma*
> *karamadhyakshaha sarva bhutadhivasaha*
> *sakshi cheta kevalo nirgunascha*

> One God hidden in all beings. All-pervading, abiding in all beings, controller of all activities. Dwelling in all beings. The witness, The enliven, The absolute beyond all attributes.

Upanishads say there are only two kinds of knowledge — the lower and the higher. Lower comprises the study of different kinds of subjects including Vedas. It is the knowledge of the world acquired through senses. Higher knowledge is direct experience of the Absolute Reality, i.e. the knowledge of the divine self. The enlightened ones do not search for God, as they know that God is everywhere. They never talk of God. Worried people talk of God.

There is no other enlightenment. We are already enlightened, as there is a great enlightened soul glowing and shining in all of us. But we are not aware of this as we are fully enveloped by worldly vices. Hence to witness the soul one should remove the envelope. It is to let off the negative vices, emotions, desires from oneself by acquired knowledge and *jnana*. The diamond is always pure and shining, but to see its shine, one should clean the dust over it. Then the glow appears.

The divine soul is the conscience and is the witness in all of us which witnesses all our actions and thoughts. One cannot escape from the view of this conscience.

Illusion of Duality

GOOD AND BAD

In this world, everywhere only goodness exists. Badness is the absence of goodness only. What we find as good may be bad to someone else. What we find good today may seem to be bad later.

HEAT AND COLD

By the power of the Sun, heat exists in this world. But there is no such thing like cold. Coolness occurs only due to lower presence of heat. Hence we have to say that it is super hot, hotter, normal hot, or little hot and so on. Any highest degrees of heat exist. For example, the heat of Corona in the Sun is as high as 3 million Kelvin degrees. Even at 0° centigrade heat exists. The lowest heat is at -273 K where heat is absent which is absolute zero. Heat is energy and we can measure heat in thermal units. We cannot measure cold. Cold is not opposite of heat. Cold is the word used for the lower presence of heat with respect to our body. The effect of feeling of heat or cold depends on the temperature of the body.

LIGHT AND DARKNESS

Light exists, but there is nothing like darkness. Darkness is not separate something. It is the absence of light only. We have Low light, Medium light, Bright light, Flash light and so on. The absence of light is called darkness. We can measure the light in luminaires and we cannot measure darkness. We can make lights and we cannot make darkness.

LIFE AND DEATH

Life exists everywhere. But death cannot exist as a substantive thing. Death is not the opposite of life. It is simply absence of life.

GOD AND EVIL

God exists everywhere. Evil is defined as man's inhuman activities like crime, violence, etc. Here evil does not exist. It is simply the result of what happens when one does not have love, understanding towards creatures and God in one's heart.

Someone is Seeing — A Story

Here is a short story of an incident that happened in a Teacher's (Guruji's) Ashram. Guruji was explaining the moral values and ethics to the disciples. He told them to be honest, truthful and straightforward in their dealings to live a peaceful life without anxieties and tensions. He also explained the existence of Reality, which is all-pervading and omnipresent.

To test the disciples one day Guruji gave a banana fruit each to the disciples and instructed them to eat the fruit secretly without anyone seeing eating the fruit. And he asked the students to report the result of this matter next morning.

On the next day the teacher asked the students how they ate the banana fruit secretly without anyone seeing. Then each student narrated a different innovative way of how they ate the fruit without anyone seeing as shown below:

- I covered my body with a dark blanket in the midnight and ate the fruit.
- I went into an abandoned hut in the nearby forest and ate.
- I hid under a cot and ate.
- I hid myself in a close paddy crop field and ate.
- I went into thick bushes and ate.
- I went into a dark cave in a hill and ate.
- I climbed a bushy tree and ate.

Like this all the students explained their ways of secretly eating the banana fruit given by the teacher. But in the same class, one student sat in a worried mood with the banana in his hand. On being asked by the teacher, this student said, "I could not eat the banana, because I could not find a secret place anywhere. Everywhere, wherever I went, I felt that God is seeing me. You taught me that God is all-pervading and lives in everyone, hence I could not find a place where no one is seeing."

By this story, one has to understand that whatever one is seeing is the manifestation of the Reality and the Reality (God) exists everywhere. We cannot hide from it, as we are a part of it. Even the very idea of hiding is known to the Reality. The Reality exists in the deep inner core of everyone of us. It is also called *satyam* — the truth.

People go to temples with a feeling that God exists in the idol in the *sanctum sanctorum*. They visit and see the idol with all hopes for fulfilment of their desires. Immediately when they come out of the temple, they forget the purpose and they start quarrelling sometimes for petty causes. This is because of ignorance and seeing God only in the images and seeing the people and the world differently.

Constant inquiry to identify the nature of the self is necessary to perceive that the Reality is within us as our very Self. We should realize that each one of us is potentially divine and the divine is within us.

14

Meditation

MEDITATION is the highest spiritual discipline. It is a repeated attempt to withdraw multiple thoughts and object in the mind and fix the mind on one thought or make the mind thoughtless. It is an act of visualizing God within oneself. It is a way to reduce the endless thoughts of mind.

The primary purpose of meditation is to become aware of the inner world of thoughts and feelings. It is the art and science of controlling the thoughts rising continuously in the mind. In meditation, one should slowly reduce the external thoughts and concentrate within oneself. This helps one to gain control and mastery over one's self gradually. By constant meditation, one slowly gains control over himself. It helps the seeker to purify the mind and thereby gain a higher level of understanding of the Reality.

Human mind is part of cosmic intelligence. The thoughts rise one after another and there is a brief gap in between two thoughts. The meditator is asked to be aware of this gap, concentrate on it and to increase the interval between thoughts for stillness of mind. This is one type of meditation.

Scriptures offer two types of knowledge. The lower comprises the knowledge of the rites and study of scriptures. The higher comprises the knowledge of the self (*atma jnan*) gained through personal experience or self-realization. Lord Krishna explained this meditation and points out three parameters to obtain the result: one-pointedness of mind, setting bounds to one's life, and evenness of vision or the state of equanimity (*sthitah prajna*).

Salvation (*moksha*) is not a state that is obtained and enjoyed after death. It consists in realizing that I am God's heir, if I am a dualist. Or I am one with God, if I am a monist.

Reading all the Vedas perfectly is not a qualification to know the truth. Hence repeating the text of the books and learning by rote may not create any effect on the reader. Highest discrimination and strong willpower with determination makes one to know the truth. Almighty is there within me, therefore I search within myself by stopping other thoughts and concentrate my mind on the reality existing within me. This is the true worship.

By one-pointed love towards Lord Krishna the single-minded and uneducated *gopika*s were able to attain oneness with the Lord. The Lord himself said, "the *gopika*s never learnt the Vedas, they never served any teacher, they practised no austerities, but by mere association with me, they attained me."

Nothing happens without human effort. We need sustained interest and unremitting efforts to bring change in our lives. We need to try our best to do anything. Everything has its own time. We need to develop patience. Some people may have to wait a bit longer than others to achieve some things in life.

We should understand the main purpose of our life. The external life that we live is not the main purpose. We should go deep into our self, which is the root cause of our personality. This inner reality witnesses whatever we do and whatever we think.

The reality exists within every being. In meditation, the

seeker can witness it directly. Meditation is real and worthy worship. It is a direct connection of seeker's mind and thoughts with the Reality. Hence it is a direct dialogue with God. Any other performances are indirect and they are rather more connected with material and adorations than application of mind. The aim of worship and spirituality is to bring a change in the mind and it is to elevate the mind. In normal worship there is a scope for the mind to escape from what the performer is doing. But in meditation the scope is less as the performer has to use his mind in meditation. Hence there is a great possibility that the mind concentrates to a single thought and gets purified.

An individual has to take off from his body, mind and senses and engage in meditation on the self. The entire life one has to meditate on the self and also perform one's duties. Meditation and devotion are to be continued even as one performs one's other duties. Without doing meditation one cannot control the thoughts and cannot elevate his mind. One should stimulate by meditation inwardly and by work and service outwardly.

Silence

Silence is a great attribute and a situation, which we must enjoy. We have to keep silent ourselves and fulfil our duties. Silence accumulates power. Silence is a great prayer and is a major requisite in meditation. It is felt that silence is dullness and inaction. But this is not true. Here silence does not mean avoiding action. But it is to bring under control the scattered and disturbed forces in us. Our thoughts and ideals work in harmony in silence. There is no friction and anxiety in silence. This is similar to working of machines. The machine, which does not have friction, makes least noise and works perfectly and lasts long.

The vehicles are already making noise by their functioning and movement. As if this is not enough, noisy music is played in some vehicles disturbing the silence and environment. There are large numbers of various sounds nowadays creating sound pollution.

We have to stop all these nonsense sounds and enjoy the sweetness of sound of silence. Someone already said the world is deafened by nonsense gossip of the people and televisions. Even the places of worship are not spared by the vice of this noise. Loudspeakers are used creating noise pollution.

Refraining from talking is not silence. Silence is making both our inner and outer vital energies calm, quiet and balanced to work in harmony. People who talk in excess are those who think less clearly. We should never talk or listen to gossip and waste our precious time. Listening to gossip is encouraging gossipers.

The greatest prayer is silence. In meditation, one has to keep the mind silent, calm, serene and the body free from motion. This is an inner quality. In deep silence, we can recognize the cosmic power. Silence conserves one's energy. It should be gradually cultivated.

The seeker can repeat a *mantra* in meditation in initial stages. Thus there will be a transition from physical to mental level and ultimately to merge the mind into consciousness.

There are two ways of practice in meditation. One is keeping the mind absent from thoughts. The other is concentrating on a single thought. Eliminating the thoughts is difficult. Hence it is better to concentrate on one image or on the Self. The concentration on a single thought eliminates other thoughts and takes one to thoughtless state.

If the solar rays are concentrated on a point by the

use of a convex lens it gets compressed energy and burns or heats the object on which the rays are focused. Like that if the mind is focused on one point it gets tremendous power.

In ordinary concentration the mind concentrates on one subject, but there are many thoughts on that one subject. But in meditation there is only one subject and only one thought.

The seeker has to know and learn meditation from a *guru* with faith and sincerity. The following are important for a practitioner: the sitting posture, witnessing the thoughts, and slowly reducing the thoughts. The sitting posture should be simple and easy to sit continuously for some considerable time.

When a beginner sits in meditation thoughts arise in the mind continuously as usual. Sometimes the thoughts become more when one sits in meditation. But one should not feel unhappy over this; just observe the thoughts as a witness.

Here we should feel that "I am the Reality (*atma*) and I am witnessing the thoughts and my body." This practice of meditation should be continued regularly in proper stipulated time selected by us. Slowly interest increases and we will like to continue to sit for more time in meditation. The thoughts and stresses will be reducing slowly. You may feel some vibrations in your body sometimes. This experience changes widely from one to another.

You should not feel that you are gaining nothing by this and may be wasting time. We are wasting much of our great precious time in most of the useless activities. Do not assess the result of your meditation. Continue it without any interruption. After some days of practice, mind starts becoming pure and it becomes calm and quiet (sattvic) in nature.

Do not raise any doubts on your meditation, sitting postures, etc. Develop faith and satisfaction on your practice of meditation and also on yourself. Severe austerity and penance are to be followed and there are no short-cuts.

Do not feel that "I am not getting concentration of mind and my thoughts are not reduced." Reduction of thoughts in mind is not that easy, because mind's nature is to think. Hence do not suppress your thoughts. Just witness them.

Also do not feel that you get some super powers by doing meditation and avoid thinking, "When do these powers come to me?"

When you sit in meditation, vent out all the negative thoughts and the stresses of the body by hypnotizing yourself like this.

- Feel that you are free from all the strain, the negative thoughts are venting out from you and your mind and body are free, lighter and calm.
- Also feel that the cosmic power is entering your head and body continuously. Feel that you are free, peaceful and happy.
- By this self-hypnotism, your mind becomes static and you can enjoy peace and calmness.

Meditation improves satisfaction, memory power, patience, concentration, mental and physical health. It decreases depression, tension, frustration, inferiority complex and psychological disorders.

By constant and continuous practice the thoughts slowly reduce. Only one thought like unshaken dripping oil remains in the mind. When the mind attains no-thoughts stage, the seeker loses his identity with the body. Then the seeker attains tremendous power dormant in the body. But it is not sudden and it is continuous and slow.

It is said, by continuous practice of meditation, the *kundalini* power, which is latent in man below the abdomen, rises and passes through the nerves and rises up stage by stage to the head. During this period meditator gets changes in the body and the mind. By continuing this practice, one may get supernatural powers (*siddhi*s). By these powers and by using his astral body one can go beyond anywhere into the space, into the universe, and into his own body without moving his physical body. He knows the past and he knows the future. He knows what others are thinking. He can disappear at one place and can appear at other place, if he desires. But the great *guru*s say that these powers are rubbish. One should not aspire for and use these powers at all. By this one becomes totally divine.

The practitioner at this stage enjoys freedom and he does not desire to live anymore in this world (*samsara*). Hence he goes to *samadhi* stage in meditation and leaves his body. His mind merges in the divinity enjoying bliss. One has to practise meditation to reduce his thoughts and to elevate his mind to higher levels and to keep him away from superstitions.

Every day one must do *pranayama*, meditation and some physical exercises or *asana*s for body fitness and health.

15

Great Inspiring Personalities

THERE is no dearth of anything in this universe including great inspiring personalities. The study of the lives of great Masters gives inspiration. We can learn and earn knowledge more than what we require. Here a few important great persons who exhibited great human values like patience, tolerance, discipline, knowledge and self-mastery are selected for narration. Living examples are always better than normal words. Hence study of great persons who overcome passions and lower propensities and who stood as a role model of complete mastery over themselves makes deep impression on us. Though we may not worship these great persons, we must emulate or atleast follow them irrespective of one's religion, caste or colour.

Sri Satya Harishchandra

King Harishchandra lived for *dharma*, truth and honesty. He experienced severe hardships in his life. He lost his family and the kingdom to stand on his one word of promise. After losing kingdom, Harishchandra worked and lived in a graveyard to earn money to pay to keep his word. He was a man with ultimate patience, truth and endurance.

Sri Rama

Sri Rama had his education from his teacher (*guru*) Vasishtha. What Rama learnt from his *guru* is well documented in the book *Yogavasishtha*. It is a great text of highest self-knowledge. Rama's character, patience, balanced talk, decision-making, practice of righteousness (*dharma*), expertise in archery, reverence to the people are exemplary. Some of the incidents from Rama's life are here described in brief, which reveal Rama's character.

Rama's stepmother Kaikeyi wanted (desired) her son Bharata to become the king of Ayodhya and wanted Rama to live in forests for fourteen years. Without any hesitation or delay Rama simply agreed to obey the command of his stepmother. The whole family of King Dasharatha and the people of the kingdom are astonished, anguished and disturbed by the desires of Kaikeyi. Except Kaikeyi all the people including her son Bharata are favouring and supporting Rama to become the king of Ayodhya. But Rama is cool, patient and accepted his stepmother's desire and left the kingdom.

Can anyone sacrifice the kingdom without any second thought if a stepmother desires?

In the history of mankind, Rama is the best example of such sacrifice. Rama's brothers including Bharata earnestly requested Rama to stop going to forests. They requested Rama to rule the kingdom. Rama can accept and heed their request. But Rama did not do so.

Can anyone withstand the temptation of the wealth and the kingdom? Rama is one and only outstanding great example of such braveness and sacrifice. Rama lived in the forest peacefully. For him there is no difference between the kingdom and the forest. Rama was already deprived of the kingdom and was living in the forests, and as if this was not enough, his wife Sita was taken away by the demon king Ravana. Rama faced all the problems with courage and equanimity.

If anyone approaches us from the land of our opponent, we do not accept that person under any circumstances. But Rama's vision, wisdom, forethought, and psychological understanding are different. He accepted Vibhishana, who was the brother of enemy Ravana, into his fold.

When Ravana was killed in the war against Rama, Vibhishana refused to perform the last rites for his dead brother Ravana, but Rama persuaded Vibhishana to do so, as it is right (*dharma*) that one must follow.

Can we imagine and do this?

After seeing Rama, demon Maricha said, If *dharma* is to take a physical form with face, hands, legs, etc. it will look like Rama. This is enough to understand Rama and to accept his greatness.

Sita

Sita's greatness lies in her accompanying Rama to live in forests. When Rama agreed to leave the kingdom and wanted to live in the forest, Sita could very well stay at Ayodhya with her in-laws. But she left everything and wanted to follow her husband Rama to live in forests.

Sita did not utter any angry word against her husband or her stepmother-in-law. She just followed Rama.

When Ravana took away Sita and when she was kept captive at Ashokavan (forest of Ashoka plants) in Ravana's kingdom Lanka, she just patiently spent her days with complete hope that her husband Rama would come and take her back.

Can any woman exhibit such great patience without any anger and hatred? Only Sita did it.

Lakshmana

In *Ramayana*, Kaikeyi wanted her son Bharata to become the king of Ayodhya instead of Rama. Lakshmana does not have any role in this matter. It is not necessary for him to accompany his brother Rama to live in forests. No one desired it. He can as well live in Ayodhya happily. But Lakshmana wanted to accompany Rama to live in forests. He accompanied and lived with Rama, faced many troubles and fought in the war against Ravana's army. Rama and Lakshmana became two indivisible and invincible brothers in the entire history. Wherever they lived, it is full of *dharma* and success.

Does any brother sacrifice life for the cause of his cousin brother? It is only one Lakshmana we can find in the entire history of mankind.

Urmila

Lakshmana's wife Urmila is too good a lady, who is so compatible and compassionate, that she allowed her husband Lakshmana to go along with Rama to the forests and bore her separation from Lakshmana with patience. Do we find any such royal lady who sacrificed her marital pleasures with her husband for the sake of others?

Bharata

Bharata was pressed and forced to become the king of Ayodhya by his mother Kaikeyi. Bharata did not desire the kingdom. He requested Rama to stay in Ayodhya and accept the coronation and the kingship. Bharata was worshipping the footwear of Rama and ruled Ayodhya under an agreement that he reigns only for fourteen years and he will die immediately if Rama does not take the kingdom from him on the day after the fourteen years are over.

Bharata does not want to get the benefit from his brother's loss. He denied the throne and ruled the kingdom as Rama's trustee in compulsion. He upheld the *dharma* and stood as dazzling figure in the history of mankind.

Do we find any such brother who wanted to leave the kingdom to his brother? Do we find any one, who after enjoying the kingdom for several years returns it to the brother?

It is only Bharata in the land of Bharat.

Hanuman

Hanuman is strong, brave and wise. He is too good at conversation and very humble. He can fight anyone alone on his own, but he is very submissive and humble. He could fight alone with Ravana and bring back Sita, but he did not do so, because it is right and appropriate for Rama to do it. Hanuman is able-bodied and can fight anyone, but he does not possess any ego about his strengths and abilities. He is always submissive and humble.

Can we find such a great person who, despite having abilities, is humble and without any ego?

Lord Krishna

Lord Krishna is all in all and all in one. He is full (*purnam*). He did a number of miracles from his childhood. He killed the demons and other kings who were against the welfare of the people, by his miraculous powers. He could fight in the Mahabharata war at Kurushetra, but he did not do so, as he promised it. Krishna drove the chariot of Arjuna during Mahabharatha war. How simple and humble he is. He is full of knowledge and he educated and motivated Arjuna to fight the war against Kauravas to establish *dharma*. *Bhagavad-Gita*, which contains Krishna's teachings to

Arjuna, is a great text containing everything for all the people irrespective of religion or creed living in any part of the world. Krishna's teachings are a must to all the people of the world. His teachings are rewritten in other words by many. Most people all over the world are following the teachings of Lord Krishna and are benefited even today. Krishna stood for *dharma* all the time.

Many people wanted and desired Krishna. Hence he had a number of wives. He managed all of them to their satisfaction. Krishna and his wives lived with pure love and worship, and not with lust and desire. Though Krishna had a number of wives he was a pure ascetic. He played different roles, each of them unique in its own way.

The great regard and worship from the people to such a great divine person as Lord Krishna is not to adorn his images and photos, but one has to become him or one must emulate him in following the path shown by him. One must sacrifice the whole mind to him.

Sri Ramakrishna Paramahamsa

There are priests in countless places of worship. But the priest at Dakshineshwar temple is totally different. He is Sri Ramakrishna Paramahamsa, who is an embodiment of Bliss (*ananda svarupa*). He lived a simple and sacred life. He developed dispassion towards wealth. He respected women. He studied Sufi and Christian religions also and realized that one could achieve same results by following those religions. He sacrificed all his powers to his disciple Narendra who was called later as Swami Vivekananda.

Sarada-ma is the wife of Sri Ramakrishna Paramahamsa. They are husband and wife for namesake only and are worshipped as divine couple.

Swami Vivekananda is a world-renowned orator and an inspirer. He was the great disciple of Sri Ramakrishna Paramahamsa. He is pure, clean and sacred. He could not tolerate the poverty and the suffering of people. He fought against blind beliefs, crude rituals and superstitions. He travelled all over the world without rest and preached the Vedanta philosophy of India. He emphasized moral education, which is the absolute need for all the people of today's society.

His speeches are highly inspiring forever. People are benefited by his speeches even today. He encouraged youth to change their ignorant and lazy attitude and urged them to awake, arise and to proceed to achieve the desired goal. Vivekananda was a dynamic and healthy person who lived as young, stayed young and died young leaving forever his inspiring speeches and Vedanta philosophy for future generations.

My humble *pranams* to all those great inspiring personalities who taught to the world an Ideal and spiritual approach to live honestly and happily by dedicating their great lives.

Bibliography

Swami Tattvavidananda Saraswati's sermons.

Chinmayananda Swami, *Meditation and Life.*

Jagatatmananda Swami, *Learn to Live* (vol. 1).

Nirvedananda Swami, *Religion and Modern Doubts.*

Ramakrishnananda Swami, *For Thinkers on Education.*

Religion columns from *The Hindu*, daily.

Upadhyaya, Amar Muni, *Bliss Discourses.*

Vedanta Kesari journal.

K. Sivananda Murthy — *Thoughts of a Seer.*

Sri Ramana Maharshi — *Upadesa Saram.*